CONVOY "MANIAC"

To,
A "V + W" DESTROYER VETERAN
" GOOD HEALTH + UP SPIRITS."
FROM THE AUTHOR,

Jim Reed H.M.S. VANOC

3-9-2002

CONVOY "MANIAC" – R.B.1

James H. Reed

The Book Guild Ltd
Sussex, England

The Book Guild Ltd.
25 High Street,
Lewes, Sussex

First published 2000
© James H. Reed 2000

Set in Times
Typesetting by
Acorn Bookwork, Salisbury, Wilts
Printed in Great Britain by
Bookcraft (Bath) Ltd. Avon

A catalogue record for this book is
available from the British Library

ISBN 1 85776 471 4

The battle of the Atlantic was the dominating factor all through the war. Never for one moment could we forget that everything happening elsewhere, on land, at sea, or in the air, depended ultimately on its outcome, and amid all other cares we viewed its changing fortunes day by day with hope or apprehension.

W. S. Churchill, *The Second World War*, Vol. V, p.6.

CONTENTS

CONTENTS

FOREWORD

In 1960 the *Sunday Pictorial* newspaper organised a war-story contest with a prize of £5,000 for the winner and £100 each for ten runners-up. They set out to find the greatest "I was there" story of them all – told by ordinary men and women at war. Brass-hats were barred. More than 6,600 startling true war stories flooded in from all parts of the world and a distinguished panel of judges selected the winners. This story was on a shortlist for awards and was included in a book of war stories published by the *Sunday Pictorial*.

Jim Reed, the author, had been a leading seaman, gunnery qualified, on an old "V & W" class destroyer HMS *Vanoc*, which had been launched in 1917 and had seen service in the great war of 1914–1918. Her duties, in September 1942, were as an escort of North Atlantic convoys based at Halifax, Nova Scotia, on which she had been engaged for long periods and had already sunk one U-boat. She also saw distinguished service in the successful evacuation of the armies at Dunkirk, and the Norwegian campaign.

The story submitted for the contest in 1960 (see chapter 2) was an "off the cuff" description of how events were seen, and not assisted by later disclosures or historical articles and declassified material. The author's title of "Decoy Convoy" was entirely his own description and may not be agreed on by those who were not there, but others in a much stronger position have believed this to be true. The author's reasoning is included and it may very well be up to the readers to judge for themselves.

1

The North Atlantic 1942

The story of Convoy R.B.1 has its background in the year 1942. On September 3rd Britain and her Allies had been engaged in war for three years. It was a year when the Battle of the Atlantic was at its most grave and critical state and indeed was to remain so for another four months into 1943. In 1942, the German U-boats were within a whisker of victory in the North Atlantic. They had destroyed and sunk almost 5.5 million tons of shipping at a cost of over 1,000 ships.

The land battles taking place in the western desert, Libya and the Middle East were not going well for the Allies and they urgently required a massive injection of more troops and munitions. This would necessitate many more cargo and troop ships and would reduce further those available in the North Atlantic. The land position took a shattering blow in June 1942 when the Allied forces at Tobruk surrendered to the Germans. Over 25,000 troops were taken as prisoners of war and considerable war materials were seized. Shipping was also desperately needed in the Middle and Far East war theatres to replenish and build up our forces and supplies. This was vital in the western desert of Africa, to be able to stop and throw back Rommel's armies advancing into Egypt and putting the Suez Canal at a high risk. Convoys of troops and supplies were coming from Australia, New Zealand, India and South Africa, and the Americans via the Panama Canal. Cargoes were being off loaded at the most convenient ports and despatched overland to the war zones. The Americans were flying their bombers direct from bases on the eastern seaboard.

On December ~~12th~~ 1941, a day of infamy, Japanese carrier-

1

borne aircraft bombed the American naval base and facilities at Pearl Harbor. Japan then declared war on America. Four days later America declared war on Germany and Italy. These declarations of war were to produce an escalation into a World War over all oceans and continents. The few countries who chose to remain neutral would also have their lives influenced by the world affairs. America – the slumbering giant – had been aroused. Her enormous production resources were put into overdrive, making her unquestionably the arsenal for democracy. This came as an enormous relief to the hard-pressed Allies at the time. The U.S.A. would be producing and contributing every type of war machines, equipment, supplies and fighting forces in enormous proportions. This would in effect enable invasions and victories in the Middle East, Europe, the Far East, Pacific and other theatres, and not least in Russia. But for some time to come it would be the Japanese who held the initiative in the Pacific and Far East, reducing the supplies of the Allies in those areas.

The Battle of the Atlantic now officially included the eastern seaboard of America. By mid January 1942, the German U-boats commenced operation *Paukenschlag*, the destruction of shipping in this area. Their successes were phenomenal, as the Americans were reluctant to adopt the convoy system, with many ships sailing independently or inadequately protected. It was not until the beginning of April that the U.S. adopted the convoy system and increased its air cover. The U-boats "Happy Time" was now at an end, and by mid July Doenitz abandoned the U.S. coast and ordered all U-boats back to the North Atlantic to concentrate on the Allied shipping.

The enormous losses of merchant ships could not be replaced by new vessels. Britain's dockyards had many ships, merchant and Naval being repaired, giving very little scope for building new ships. At the end of 1942 there was a shortfall of over one million tons between merchant ships lost and new ships being built. This was an industry to which the German bombers gave priority, attacking ports, dockyards and installations, and very few escaped. Even with the U.S. vast shipbuilding industry at full production and the first "Liberty"

2

ship the *Patrick Henry* being commissioned, it was not until July 1943 that the new Allied shipping tonnage overtook the losses. This was then considered the turning point of the Atlantic struggle.

But in 1942 the Battle of the Atlantic was at its worst and what was most serious, merchant shipping was in crisis at the beginning of the year. Russia and America were pressurising Britain to start a second front across the English Channel in the summer of 1942 to reduce the enormous pressure German forces were applying on the Russian fronts. Churchill and service chiefs would be unable to sanction such a vast operation on an enemy so well prepared until the enormous amount of war machines, supplies and men were available, trained and ready. The attack on Germany and her fortress captive countries was continuing with R.A.F. and U.S. day and night bombing raids on the vital industrial and shipbuilding areas in a meticulous and prolonged softening up of German industrial power. It was stated that "Bomber Harris" the Air Chief Marshall was convinced that bombing alone would make Germany surrender, without invasion. It was this dedication by Churchill and his airchiefs and their priority use of all aircraft that had tragically left the "Black Pit", the North Atlantic 300 square miles "Air Gap", for so long, allowing the U-boats to concentrate their patrols and wolfpacks there, immune to any attacks by coastal command aircraft. It was indeed another tragedy when statistics showed the results from the bombing of the U-boat yards and installations during this period, that with the thousands of tons of bombs dropped and great losses of Allied bombers, the numbers of U-boats built and commissioned were unaffected, and the German programmes and specified targets were achieved.

Any invasion had to be vitally dependent on the state of the shipping reserves. Early in 1942, the Americans introduced operation "Bolero" to ascertain the build up of U.S. forces and supplies to the United Kingdom. One of the main considerations was how to overcome the shipping crisis and to increase the shipping reserves available. This at a time when the U-boat campaign was steadily decreasing the ships in the

3

North Atlantic by an average of 84 ships a month, almost three ships a day during 1942. The Americans were investigating in depth all the ships available for cargoes of war materials, also ships being used for internal and domestic services. These ships had been designed for coastal and river waters, carrying goods and passengers from port to port mostly on the eastern seaboard. These vessels would be examined and graded and if suitable, would be structurally improved for deep sea and ocean journeys. Those whose design and structures would not be suitable for the Atlantic weather conditions would be retained and utilised for the large movements of troops, supplies and workers required to maintain an internal structure. The present troopships capacity was to be further increased by packing in more troops and the use of the "monster liners". With their high speeds they would cross the Atlantic either independently or in small groups or two or three. This was considered the most efficient method for quick crossings, reducing the dangerous time at sea.

Merchant ships' cargoes across the North Atlantic were given top priority for war materials of every type. Other goods and food had a lesser priority, resulting from time to time in a reduction of the people's food rations and the disappearance altogether of all imported fresh fruit and non essentials, also some types of fuel. The other war areas would also find a reduction in their volume of shipping.

It should not go unnoticed that in February 1942, the President of the United States set in motion what was to be the greatest shipbuilding programme in world history. The American war shipping administration was to be the official body to organise a target by the end of 1942 of 24 million tons of new ships, that is about 750 ships in 1942 and 1,500 in 1943. By the end of the war over 100 new shipyards had been built with over 1.5 million workers and many ships were built by the revolutionary mass production techniques of Henry J. Kaiser.

The American lend-lease agreement started in 1940 when 50 old U.S. destroyers were released to Britain in return for granting U.S. leases on naval bases on Bermuda, Jamaica, Trinidad, British Guyana and Newfoundland. This was to open a flood gate for the enormous quantities of war materials that would be needed before an Allied final victory was accomplished. The destroyers that had been negotiated for during a meeting between Churchill and Roosevelt were to help in the escorting of the Atlantic convoys which up to that time were suffering due to the shortage of escorts from day one and the commitments of the Royal Navy in the dark days of 1940.

In 1942, the U.S. "war shipping administration" had requisitioned 11 American passenger steamers which had plied their trade in coastal and river waters. In July 1942, these 11 ships were transferred to the British M.W.T. (Ministry of War Transport) under the lend-lease agreement and their future role was described as for use in the European war area, as hospital and accommodation ships. Three of these ships were not to make this hazardous Atlantic crossing at the most vulnerable time of the U-boat battles: *John Cadwalader* (total loss by fire at Philadelphia August 29th 1942); *Colonel J.A.Moss* (at Halifax N.S. found unsuitable); *Virginia Lee* (also found unsuitable). This reduced the number of ships to eight to form Convoy R.B.1., code named "Maniac", or known to the Americans as "The Honeymoon Fleet", in honour of the thousands of honeymoon couples who had used their services. These eight ships were mustered into a convoy for movement to Europe. This convoy, assuredly one of the most remarkable of the war, sailed on September 21st 1942. One might have expected a collection of middle-aged boats to be a poor match for German submarines. A German wolfpack encountered the convoy five days out of St John's N.F. and was able to sink the *Boston*, *New York* and *Yorktown*. The rest of the little fleet survived but none ever managed to be restored to her peacetime duties. The *President Warfield* eventually perished in the Eastern Mediterranean as the *Exodus* in 1947, after carrying illegal immigrants into Palestine, far from her haunts on Chesapeake Bay.

2

The Decoy Convoy?

Convoy Name: R.B.1 C.T.F24. (Honeymoon)
Code Name: "Maniac"

This story covers just a few days – a little more than a week –
but the events of that short period late in September 1942 and
the start of an early winter in the North Atlantic must forever
be remembered by those who survived the crossing, and were
extremely lucky to do so. At the same time we remember those
who paid the supreme price.

As far as the escorts are concerned, the events started at
Halifax, Nova Scotia, Canada. This harbour had been vastly
and efficiently developed from a comparatively small area to a
large and vital base to shelter convoys and naval ships in
preparation for the hazards of the North Atlantic traffic. The
facilities catered well for the numerous destroyers, frigates,
corvettes and escort vessels of all Allied Navies which carried
out the long tedious tasks of escorting valuable convoys of
men, arms, equipment, food, etc across the Atlantic to the
U.K. Most of the escorts operated to midway rendezvous
where they changed over with escorts operating from the U.K.
coast. Some escorts would complete full crossings but others
would find their fuel supplies far too difficult to maintain a
constant escort and carry out all the extra mileage of attacking
U-boats, picking up survivors and steaming at high speeds to
rejoin the convoys. The North Atlantic was the prize hunting
ground for the German U-boat packs – like wolves just
waiting to kill any ship they could get their sights on. At this
time of the war every ship that left for England was vital

6

whatever its cargo, and even ships with no cargo were vital as you will see.

The quays of Halifax had a few of these convoy escorts tied up side by side, some having a boiler clean, others being repaired, ammunitioning or provisioning etc, all in readiness for the next turn of duty. Practically all these ships wore that well worked look that comes only from days and weeks continuously fighting fog, gales and rough weather which can be experienced in the North Atlantic on convoy duty. Paint was worn off, and the grey paint nearly white from the salt. Two such ships that day were the old "V & W" class destroyers the *Vanoc* and the *Veteran*, both about 25 years old, but still very sound and ideal efficient ships for the job, although not so much for comfort. There was always a good comradeship between these ships' crews when on shore leave or alongside, sometimes sharing a session of tombola, a smoke or a yarn.

The crew of the *Vanoc*, cleaning up after a spell of convoying, watched as the "Old Man" Commander Churchill crossed one or two ships to come back on board after a visit to Naval HQ ashore. Needless to say a few good-natured remarks passed round the lads: "What's he volunteered for now" and so on. Of course these remarks were always made discreetly enough for the "old man" to hear every word, but he never let on, although he must have chuckled inwardly. Every man respected him. He was one of the old breed of no nonsense Naval Commanders and was old enough to be the father of most of us. Also he could suffer sea-sickness with the best of us. Shortly after the Captain's arrival on board, the Bosun's mate piped "clear lower deck, fall in aft", an order reserved for very rare and special occasions. The response was immediate, and in no time a tightly packed circle was formed around the Captain who was standing on a hatch. No dock workers were allowed on board, just the crew alone.

The Captain then proceeded in as few words as possible to tell us that the *Veteran* and ourselves, *Vanoc*, were to go back home to the U.K., that a few hours' shore leave would be taken in two watches for shopping purposes and above all not to mention anything to anyone ashore. (Strict secrecy was an accepted fact throughout the service but we always were reminded – "Careless talk costs lives".)

The crew soon carried out their shopping, making certain that no farewells were mentioned, and returned on board ship. The strange thing most of us encountered ashore was the fact that so many people seemed to know we were off home with a convoy. 'Some secret!' most of us thought. (In recent years the son of Captain J. Murray of the *Naushon* wrote to me as follows: "Although their departure from St. John's was supposed to be highly secret a local barber cutting his hair could give it to him exactly, sometime before sailing.")

However, the ship had to be prepared for sea and every man-jack of us had plenty to do. Cables securely lashed, boats, rafts and all gear carried on deck, doubly certain that nothing was likely to be lost when we started shipping the seas on board. This was a very common occurrence as the deck was only a few feet above the sea. Below decks there was the same routine, everything which moved had to be made safe. As regards our shore clothes, these were neatly folded up and wrapped in paper or similar and put in lockers ready for the next shore leave – where or when we didn't know. Out came the sea gear, an indifferent assortment of clothes. Civilian shirts and jackets, fur and woollen headgear, balaclavas, sea boots and all types of sea-boot socks – most represented football clubs – oilskins, duffels, gloves and everything possible. Practically no two men dressed alike, but all were well dressed to keep out the cold and wet weather. Warmth and comfort was preferred to smartness on these boats at sea, and we often remarked what our mates on the "Big 'Uns" would have to say if they saw us. I seem to remember the Old Man dressed in a battered corduroy jacket at times, but I couldn't swear if his gold braid was sewn on.

One serious and main factor to be considered by these escort ships crossing the North Atlantic was the need for maximum oil fuel. The water tank which was used for washing, cleaning etc had to be sacrificed for fuel to give extra endurance. This left one small tank of fresh water, about 1,500 gallons for food and drink only, no luxuries like washing or shaving or cleaning. The only access to this water was a small tank in the galley which was restricted to meal times, and the stopcock locked.

Needless to say similar preparations were being carried out by the *Veteran*. It must be remembered that the complement of these very overcrowded ships could be up to 170 officers and men which gave no leeway in the efforts to conserve fresh water and indeed fuel oil, over several days in appalling weather.

The convoy, at that time called "Honeymoon" – remembering the thousands of American honeymoon couples who had sailed on these ships in peace-time – left Halifax at 1100 on Wednesday September 16th 1942, bound for St John's Newfoundland. The convoy consisted of the eight ships mentioned, but the original convoy was to have been 11 ships. However one was totally destroyed by fire and two were found unsuitable for a deep sea crossing. At the given sailing time *Vanoc* and *Veteran* slipped their mooring and with screws turning got under way with the usual good-hearted remarks from our sister escorts ringing in our ears. As we cleared harbour and approached the open sea we saw for the first time the convoy we were to escort home to the U.K.

The first stage of the voyage to St. John's Newfoundland was uneventful, arriving on September 18th. It was then that a crucial decision was made by the Naval HQ which with hindsight may have contributed to the disaster that followed. It seems that initially the 11 river boats were to form part of a larger convoy, being partly obscured in a central position. Some doubts were expressed that their speeds of 13.5 knots would be sufficient to keep up with a fast convoy. The next decision was that the final eight ships would sail directly to Iceland with the two-destroyer escort and be later re-routed to the U.K. The final decision was influenced by the senior escort commander whose report suggested that after what he had experienced in the ships' passage from Halifax to St. John's, they should sail directly to Londonderry. This suggestion was confirmed by the Fleet Officer Newfoundland on the 19th of September.

Prior to departure from St. John's, the escort commanders and ships' captains attended a briefing at Naval HQ. At this meeting the official name of the convoy became R.B.1, the previous name "Honeymoon" became obsolete. The code name became convoy "Maniac". At that time Captain Beckett said that although the code word was very appropriate, he considered it should be in the plural. (One can only wonder who could sardonically and cynically suggest such a name.)

Monday September 21st 1942

Convoy R.B.1 "Maniac" departed from St John's Newfoundland at 1400 on Monday September 21st, formed into three columns, a total of eight ships with a two-destroyer escort. To the seasoned crews of convoy escorts of all types of cargo and troop transports, the eight ships of R.B.1 presented something we had not seen before, not cargo ships, but ships of a high superstructure, two with twin funnels and the others with high single funnels. From a distance, in a haze or at night, a U-boat periscope just above sea level could quite easily recognise these ships as large troopships, some resembling our more famous liners. This illusion was soon shattered as we came closer and saw that they were in fact coastal or river pleasure boats. By no stretch of the imagination would any seafarer consider them to be suitable for an Atlantic crossing near winter. However someone had, and all the ships had undergone considerable work to "whaleback" with heavy timbers the most vulnerable parts of the superstructures, enclosing completely the large windows and open deck spaces, also constructing some gun positions. Some carried on deck many drums of oil. It now became known that these ships carried no cargo, no passengers, in ballast, to reduce the top hamper and it later emerged that they were manned entirely by volunteers from Coastlines Shipping, Liverpool who had come over to the U.S. on the *Queen Mary*, 550 officers and men.

It seemed unbelievable to consider sending such frail and minimum-draught vessels across the Atlantic at that time of

10

the year or to send them at all. 1942 was a year when the ships and supplies being convoyed from the American and Canadian ports to the U.K. were at their most vulnerable. North Atlantic ship losses for 1942 were just over 1,000 ships and a tonnage of almost 5.5 million. The September figures reached 95 ships lost, averaging three a day and these were vital cargoes of food, arms and men to sustain our country and build up the enormous reserves required. September was also the month of special endeavour as Operation "Torch", the landings in North Africa, was a priority and would be carried out in November.

Tuesday September 22nd 1942

The rest of Monday September 21st after our departure from St. John's, and Tuesday 22nd were uneventful with the convoy maintaining its course and speed and carrying out the specified zig-zag patterns. The escort ships' crews were at their stations in watches, but it was common practice and the natural thing to do for those off watch and present on the open decks to be keeping a look-out also. At this time in 1942, it was vital that convoys and escorts were given as much information as possible of U-boats, surface ships and aircraft of the enemy, to enable defensive activities. The source of this information came mainly from detecting signals being made by U-boats, by HF/DF (high frequency direction finding). This was a British invention to detect the radio transmissions of German U-boats at sea, primarily in the North Atlantic battles. Skilled operators on escorts fitted with HF/DF could detect within 20 miles. There were many HF/DF shore stations fully operational covering all areas and they passed the information to main intelligence centres. Washington D.C. was the HQ of COMINCH – CinC U.S. Fleet – and it was there that all information was gathered, analysed, plotted and signalled to the convoys and escorts concerned. The continuous, very highly secret, code breaking of the very sophisticated "Triton" enigma machines was a massive task and although not 100%

11

successful, intelligence could obtain information to enable near miraculous predictions. This operation of code breaking was being carried out in the U.S. and Britain with remarkable success, but known only to very few people throughout the war.

The first signal from COMINCH to the *Vanoc* and also to the escorts of other convoys in the area gave a U-boat position by DF at 2309 on Tuesday September 22nd, over 150 miles, position 49.50 N 45 W Enigma. So it was that convoy R.B.1 had arrived in the lair of the German U-boat wolf packs less than 36 hours after sailing from St. John's. Between Tuesday 22nd and Saturday 26th, *Vanoc* received at least 29 U-boat positions in the area and 10 reports of U-boats making sighting reports of a convoy or important unit. A position report of a surface enemy ship did not materialise. All these reports received by *Vanoc* and convoys in the area ranged between 54.20 N and 58.40 N and 18.50 W and 38.10 W. The ships were sailing in four columns. The Commodore was leading ship in the second port column and the Vice Commodore was leading ship in the port column.

Wednesday September 23rd 1942

R.B.1 convoy was sighted and reported by U-404 (Von Bulow), U-380 (Rother) and U-91 (Walkerling) all from group *Vorwarts* on patrol in the area, indicating a fast convoy and assumed to be a special troop transport convoy. B.D.U., the German U-boat command receiving all U-boat signals, instructed the *Vorwarts* group of 10 U-boats to close and engage, also group *Pfiel* of seven U-boats to proceed to the scene on completion of operations against convoy S.C.100.

The Germans were completely fooled by the ships' profile, and considered the convoy so important that the high command sent 17 U-boats to attack. On this day the *Vanoc* Commander Churchill, sent the following signal to CinC Western Atlantic:

12

R.B.1 was shadowed from ahead all last night and suspect shadowing continues today Thursday 24th. Escort have insufficient fuel to carry out putting down sweep. Evasive tactics proved useless in extreme visibility with full moon. Air cover would be appreciated as soon as possible. 53.14 N 35.20 W course 074, 12 knots.

Also on the 23rd, the Commodore, Captain R.S. Young, on board the *Boston* signalled to the convoy: "Submarines in the vicinity", and again on the 24th he signalled: "U-boat shadowed convoy, expect an attack during the night".

Thursday September 24th

An urgent U-boat warning, sent from COMINCH to *Vanoc*: "U-boat estimated your vicinity by DF at 0916/24 had made sighting report of convoy or important unit." The convoy formed into single line abreast during the day. There were no known attacks on the 24th but further signals of U-boat positions came in.

By now the escort ships had been at action stations for some hours and would remain so for some days, food and drink would have to be brought to all stations when possible and safe to do so. The convoy crews would be in a similar state and the gun crews (some guns had been installed in these ships during the preparations to cross the North Atlantic) would be at action stations throughout. As for the escort commanders, ships' captains and all crews, there was no doubt in their minds that the German U-boat command were carefully planning the total destruction of this convoy which they were convinced was a special troop transport containing ships of the *Queen Mary* class and others identified as the *Viceroy of India*, *Reina del Pacifico* and *Derbyshire*. It was now a plain case of waiting at the Germans' convenience. The advantage and strength to attack was entirely theirs. In this area of the North Atlantic they had no worries from aircraft attacks. This was

13

the "Black Hole" – among other names – in the mid Atlantic which was out of range of the types of coastal command aircraft operating, and ideal for the U-boat packs. With hindsight, this should not have been the case, as the Allies had VLRs – very long range aircraft – capable of closing this gap, but those in power designated all these aircraft to bomber command after repeated requests by coastal command. Eventually President Roosevelt intervened in March 1943 to supply VLR Liberators and by mid April 1943 the "Air Gap" was closed and 41 VLRs were operating.

Friday September 25th 1942

In the early morning – the middle watch – 0158 hours, *Vanoc's* ASDIC operator detected a strong contact as a U-boat. *Vanoc* carried out two attacks with patterns of depth charges in position 53.52 N 31.46 W. The contact was lost after the second attack, *Vanoc* having to rejoin the convoy in haste. COMINCH confirmed to *Vanoc* that a previous signal of a U-boat's sighting report was indeed on Convoy R.B.1. The German reports for the day and night of 24/25th September give a total of eight U-boats in contact with R.B.1 making three unsuccessful attacks:

U-91 (Walkerling) was attacked, forced to submerge and lost contact with the convoy.
U-96 (Helriegel) and U-380 (Rother) were experiencing engine trouble reducing their speeds to get ahead of the convoy.
U-410 (Sturm) and U-584 (Deecke) were attacked by the escorts and forced away from the convoy.
U-260 (Purkhold) unsuccessful attack and lost contact.
U-211 (Hauser) fired a double miss at a twin-funnelled steamer.
U-607 (Mengerson) was depth charged after an underwater attack.

This negative success by eight U-boats on this extra ordinary convoy over a day or so was of course unknown to the convoy and escorts and only came to light in later articles after the war ended. It shows what the convoy was up against, but this phenomenal luck just couldn't last. On Friday 25th, 14 U-boats had reported being in contact with the convoy and at 1337 local time, the U-boat U-216 (Schultz) attacked the twin-funnelled ship SS *Boston*, hitting her with two torpedoes on her port side, blowing her to pieces. She sank in about seven minutes. One hit was on the port quarter and one on the port bow. Four lifeboats were seen to have got away. The *New Bedford* allocated as the rescue ship proceeded to pick up survivors. The chief officer Mr H.F.W. Kaye, in charge of lowering a boat, was killed when the boat caught underneath the belting and capsized throwing him into the water. It turned out that only two survivors boarded the rescue ship, the others making for the *Veteran* which lay much lower in the water. Signalman Ray Freeman, 19 years old and on his first ship, on duty on the bridge of the *Vanoc* recalls the Captain ordering the ship to stop for only seven seconds to pick up any survivors. There was a fairly heavy swell. Only three survivors were seen and they were dragged out of the sea in about three seconds (or so it seemed). An unconfirmed report gave the *Veteran* saving 48 survivors including the Commodore from the *Boston*. The complement was 64 men. The *Boston* sank in position 54.23 N 27.54 W, German grid AK6656. At this point the convoy scattered. The *Yorktown* sighted two torpedo tracks approaching her and with the helm hard over to starboard watched one torpedo passing across her bow 30 feet ahead and another about 15 feet astern. The *President Warfield* opened fire at the torpedoes with her 12-pounder and oerlikon guns.

About four hours after the *Boston* sank, the convoy was reformed, with Captain C. Mayers, SS *New York*, in charge as Vice Commodore, proceeding in four columns at 9 knots and zig-zag pattern. At about 2000 local time the *Yorktown's* steering gear became fouled on the drum of the steering engine and she stopped for repairs. *Vanoc* returned to see what was wrong but had to get back to the convoy when told the repair would take some hours.

By 2200 on the 25th the steering gear was repaired. Captain

N.G. Boylan made a decision not to keep to the convoy track but to steer north for about 30 miles and at 2330 on the 25th to alter course and pick up the stragglers' route. While the repair work was being carried out, the *Yorktown* crew observed, about 15 miles ahead, starshells, snowflake rockets and red lights, also the shudder of two powerful explosions presumed to be depth charges. When the *Northland* was returning to reform the convoy, and leaving the *Vanoc* and *New Bedford* astern, a U-boat surfaced about 1,500 yards off her port bow at about 2045 on the 25th. She opened fire with the 12-pounder and oerlikon guns with possible hits. The U-boat crash dived.

The *Southland* was also in the thick of the action, as the ships were being signalled to reform by the Vice Commodore. Twenty minutes after retaining her course she sighted a U-boat periscope 200–300 yards off the starboard beam. Avoiding action swung the ship round and she carried out violent zig-zagging and speed alterations. The ship opened fire and expended 14 rounds of 12-pounder before losing sight of the U-boat. Shortly after, the gunners sighted a periscope on the port quarter and fired a further 18 rounds. The U-boat disappeared from view and was not seen again. After these incidents the convoy slowed down and stood on at a speed of 7–8 knots to enable the rescue ship *New Bedford* and the two escorts to catch up.

Also during the action the helm on the *Naushon* jammed and she proceeded to go round in circles until repaired at about 1425, then proceeding after the convoy. The convoy escorts rejoined the convoy at about 1830, reformed with seven ships, single line abreast, *Veteran* to port, *Vanoc* to starboard zig-zag pattern, mean course 081 speed 9 knots.

Later signals by aldis lamp were as follows:

Veteran to *Vanoc*: Suggest we change stations as you seem to be getting all the action and getting short of depth charges.
Vanoc to *Veteran*: I agree and am short of fuel, I will take station ahead and you astern.

The next attack came at 2057/25, local time. U-96 (Hellriegel)

16

attacked the second of the two twin-funnelled ships, SS *New York*, Vice Commodore Captain C. Mayers, the sister ship of the *Boston*. The torpedoes caused a heavy explosion and fires started, possibly from the oil tanks. She remained afloat for some time but sank in a further attack. Her position was 54.34 N 25.44 W, German grid AL4483. The convoy became disorganised and scattered. The escorts fired flares to force the U-boats to submerge out of sight. *Veteran* stood by to pick up survivors. *Vanoc* proceeded to attempt to reform and protect the remaining six ships in darkness. *Veteran* reported she was proceeding to rejoin convoy and she had 28 survivors aboard. The look-outs on the *Vanoc* were continuously searching for tell-tale signs of periscopes, and U-boats were blatantly signalling to each other information to attack. Further unsuccessful attacks were reported by U-91, U-356, U-404 and U-410.

Saturday September 26th

At 0736 local time came the next success for the U-boats. In position 54.34 N 25.44 W, German grid reference AL5472, U-404 (Von Bulow) sighted *Veteran* and fired a spread of three torpedoes. Two found the target. She blew up and must have sunk in seconds with no survivors. *Vanoc* was at this time far over the horizon attempting to reform the convoy which had previously been instructed to steer 081 and reform at daybreak, with no success. HMS *Veteran* (Lieutenant Commander T.H.Garwood) had a complement of nine officers and 150 men and was believed to be carrying 28 survivors from the *New York* and 48 from the *Boston*.

Vanoc had previously sent a signal reporting the sinking of the *New York*. The convoy was disorganised in the attack. Broadcast instructions were to steer 081 and reform at daylight. The fuel situation of the escort was becoming shaky.

Also a signal had been sent from CinC West Atlantic to HMS *Sabre*, HMS *Scimitar* and HMS *Saladin*:

Escort O.N.132, 20th ES. FR. If you have completed with

fuelling, proceed reinforcement R.B.1 in 54.23 N 27.54 W at 1340zed 25th routed through 54.51 N 25.01 W and 55.31 N 17.59 W, speed 12 knots, report action taken.

At 1000 hours on Saturday September 26th *Vanoc* sighted a single ship ahead and identified her as the *President Warfield* on mean course 081, zig-zagging, speed 15 knots. At the same time *Saladin* and *Scimitar* were sighted and after signals, the two proceeded to escort her and were later joined by *Vanoc*. A coastal command aircraft – now in range – arrived and was asked to search for *Veteran* with no success. Also the *Veteran* was signalled to break WT silence and report her position, again with no reply.

To the crew of *Vanoc* coming out of the night action, all that was seen of the convoy was this single-funnel ship and many thought that the two of us were the only survivors. However, the Germans had not given up yet, although many of the 17 U-boats had been outpaced and left behind. The *Yorktown* had decided to leave the convoy in position 55.10 N 18.50 W, grid reference AL6527, sailing independently 12.5 knots at 081 at 2025 on September 26th. She was sighted by the U-boat U-619 (Makowski) about 300 miles from Tory Island, an area covered by aircraft of Coastal Command and not too safe for U-boats. The U-boat attacked, obtaining a torpedo hit on the port side immediately underneath the bridge. This caused a complete collapse of all the superstructure of the wooden bridge and everything forward, the engines stopped and the ship tore itself apart and sank within three minutes. The survivors in the water in extremely difficult conditions managed to man four rafts and a waterlogged boat they had managed to right and bale out. These survivors had to endure this ordeal from 2025 on Saturday September 26th until 1900 on Monday September 28th when they were picked up by the destroyer *Sardonix* after being sighted at 1200 on Sunday the 27th, probably by a VLR Liberator. SS *Yorktown* (Captain W.P. Boylan) had a complement of 62 men; 18 men lost their lives.

So, with hindsight, and completely unknown at the time, the state of Convoy "Maniac" on the night of Saturday September

Holmside.

I) 5613293

Launched 20/4/42

cor 77 CC

Redhead Safety SShields

26th was: one destroyer escort HMS *Vanoc*, five river boats, *Northland, Southland, President Warfield, New Bedford and Naushon*. And losses of HMS *Veteran*, SS *Boston, New York* and *Yorktown*. Loss of life 302 souls.

With the remainder of the convoy now dispersed and sailing independently the ships proceeded as follows: *President Warfield, Northland* and *Naushon* made it to Londonderry: *Southland* and *New Bedford* made it to the Clyde. Some of the ships were convinced that they were being followed most of the way home by U-boats and also picking up their signals. The *Vanoc* in company with *Saladin* and *Scimitar* made landfall at Mouille, County Donegal. She replenished fuel, ammunition, depth charges and supplies and later was engaged in convoys for Operation "Torch", but that belongs to another story.

Other activity at the time

As previously mentioned there was a great deal of other convoy activity during the passage of Convoy R.B.1. Convoy S.C.100 Nova Scotia to the U.K., 24 ships and in excess of six escorts were located by U-boats on September 18th. An initial six U-boats were augmented by three more and then eight more called in. Stormy weather prevented some U-boats reaching the convoy but after five days of attacks five ships had been sunk between September 20th and 24th 1942, these being *Empire Hartebeeste, Tennessee, Athelsultan, Penmar* and *Roumanie*. S.C.100 was a slow east-bound convoy. Speed made great difficulty for the U-boats to keep up and they were re-directed to R.B.1 on September 23rd. The pursuit of S.C.100 was finally broken off on September 25th, bad weather prevailing. Convoy O.N.131, westbound, and Convoy H.X.208, westbound were also in the general area. Convoy S.C.102 sailed from New York on September 19th.

Another highly secret crossing around this time was by the RMS *Queen Mary*, one of the monster troop liners, carrying 11,000 American soldiers to the U.K. At 1412 hours on October 2nd 1942 she collided with HMS *Curocoa*, which was sliced in two and sunk. 331 men out of 430 crew perished. The ships' position at the time was 55.50 N 08.38 W off north west Ireland. She had left New York on September 27th. U-407, after leaving R.B.1, sighted the *Queen Mary* on October 1st 1942 and made an unsuccessful attack on her.

After the continuous U-boat attacks on Convoy R.B.1 it was later confirmed that 17 U-boats had been involved. The two escort destroyers were facing an almost impossible task of trying to keep the convoy together, protecting them as the ships sailed further apart, rescuing survivors and attacking the U-boat contacts, while at the same time seriously short of fuel. Both escorts were fully aware that if they stopped their ship for only a few seconds they would be presenting a sitting target, ideal for the lurking U-boats and requiring several minutes before they could regain a manoeuvrable speed. Yet these two escorts and the rescue ship *New Bedford* carried out this dangerous task time and time again. It is almost certain that the *Veteran* was blown up during her last rescue mission.

In later months of 1942, and in the following years, there were strong rumours that Convoy R.B.1, code name "Maniac", was indeed a decoy convoy to attract and lure as many U-boats as possible from the more vital and important convoys.

During this period in 1942, and indeed all of 1942, the North Atlantic convoy shipping was in crisis. The losses of ships were reaching unacceptable levels, over 1,000 in 1942, and even with every effort being made by the Allied ship builders to build new ships and repair others, there was no sign that the gap was closing. The German U-boat CinC had withdrawn virtually all U-boats from the South Atlantic and sent them to reinforce those in the North Atlantic. The Germans were also now using special U-boats as oil tankers, enabling longer patrols. In spite of the heavy Allied bombing of the German occupied ports, U-boat bases and construction areas, there was no decline in their new U-boat launching programme. The Atlantic air gap, the area that was out of range by Coastal Command aircraft from both sides of the Atlantic was no nearer to being closed, with no VLR aircraft available.

Convoy cargoes were geared up to war materials and fuel. Only essential goods were carried, hence further food rationing was a possibility. And most secret and important was the preparation for the American invasion of North Africa – Operation "Torch" – which was planned for November 1942.

The U-boat war in the North Atlantic was only a whisker from complete success. It would seem that to send a convoy of eight frail river boats and two of the Royal Navy's oldest destroyers across the North Atlantic on a course that was well known as an area dominated by strong U-boat patrols was to say the least strange, and perhaps more devious. In the transfer of these ships, it was assumed they would be used in an invasion of Europe as possible hospital ships, accommodation ships for training and so on. But these ships would need a lot of work done to them, to strip back their Atlantic cladding and redesign them for their future roles. Was this possible at a time when the ship repair and building industries in the U.K. were snowed under with work, and when would they be used? Would the danger endured and loss of ships and lives compensate for the roles the ships would later carry out? There must have been many damaged ships or hulks in the U.K. at that time, quite capable of conversion. Even with the utmost secrecy it was known that the invasion of Europe was some time away, after all this was September 1942.

What was accomplished? The profile of the ships, high superstructure, high funnels, two of them with twin funnels, completely fooled the U-boats and the German U-boat command. All reports described them as an important convoy of large troop transports including ships of the *Queen Mary* class. Ships lost had been falsely identified as the SS *Viceroy of India*, SS *Reina Del Pacifico* and SS *Derbyshire*, and even the U-boats failed to follow up a sinking to find evidence of a heavy troopship.

The German command was cock-a-hoop with this tremendous success. Even the bombastic propaganda minister Herr Goebels in a broadcast on Berlin Radio, gloated about the U-boats' destruction of this large troop convoy, claiming heavy losses among the "ships of the *Queen Mary*" class and said,

'The defence was so fierce that it could not be observed whether two or more of the ships was sunk.'

But perhaps even this statement does not come up to a military commentary broadcast in English from Calais on October 3rd 1942, between a German announcer and a Captain Bauer:

Captain Bauer – It's no small achievement, really, to stick to a convoy in a U-boat which has to travel a large part of the way under water and has to manoeuvre a lot to get into the most favourable position.

Announcer – Are you referring to that latest convoy, consisting of fast troop transporters, of which three were sunk?

Captain Bauer – Yes, the one of which British authorities are so reluctant to admit that it fell to our U-boats. It is marvellous that those fast moving vessels, zigzagging along under heavy protection, would be pursued for days and, finally, three of them sunk and two more damaged. It must have been very hard to catch them. But let us acknowledge that it must also be very hard for the British Admiralty to admit these losses, for they show all too blatantly the emptiness of their claim to have mastered the U-boat danger, while the admission would throw a bad light on the difficulties of transporting large bodies of troops across the ocean.

Propaganda of course, but interesting. So what is clear is that 17 U-boats were drawn away from their patrol positions over several days to an unimportant convoy which had no great significance to the vital side of the war effort, leaving other gaps and areas less hazardous to other convoys.

3

The Author's Opinion

The story of Convoy "Maniac", R.B.1 was published in small extracts in various magazines and journals in the U.K., America and Canada, soon after the end of World War II. These items were obviously similar in their basic interpretation, but now, with more available unclassified information, it is possible to look again at the circumstances of this most unusual North Atlantic convoy in September 1942.

I was there at the time, serving on the only surviving escort HMS *Vanoc*. I have always had misgivings about the true reason for this convoy and am in disagreement with what has been accepted of its story.

First, you must remember that the year was 1942 and the month September, the start of the season of equinoctial gales. What was more important, it was in 1942 and the latter months that the North Atlantic convoy system was at its most grave time, and only a whisker away from total collapse and destruction. Over 1,000 merchant ships were sunk in ~~that~~ ~~September~~ and the German U-boat command had withdrawn U-boats from other areas to concentrate on the destruction of the North Atlantic convoy system. Over 160 U-boats were operating in the Atlantic.

Two more serious setbacks must also be considered: The Black Hole, an area of over 300 square miles of the convoy routes, had no air cover and gave the U-boats an enormous advantage of being able to press home their attacks. The other setback was the fact that in about April 1942 the first German milch-cows entered the Atlantic. These oil tanker U-boats, lying some 500 miles north-west of Bermuda, could refuel

23

Correction
Page 23. Lines 17 & 18 - Change 'that September', to read 'in 1942'

many U-boats, avoiding their return to bases in France and Germany and providing a very high operational efficiency. In August, 21 out of 63 convoys were attacked with heavy losses of shipping, even more on the North American seaboard, especially in the Caribbean and the St. Laurence estuary. Vital shipping and indeed escort ships were lost, with no chance of replacement, so there was a drain on the number of ships available.

The United States had some time earlier instituted a lend-lease agreement with the U.K., exchanging 50 old destroyers for bases in the West Indies and various British Colonies. After some more repairs, alterations and maintenance these ships were made ready to carry out the vital role of escort duties. At the entry of America to World War II Operation "Bolero" was introduced. This was the plan to build up the U.S. Army and supplies in the U.K. Troopship capacity was increased by one third. Cargo carrying capacity had become so scarce that exports were given a low priority, leading from time to time to further food rationing in the U.K., the disappearance of fresh fruit and huge reductions in meat and butter. The rations of food in 1942 were averaging 3,000 calories per head per day but the main survival foods, flour, meats, fats and sugar, all of which depended mostly on imports, were down to only four months' supplies.

For the Allies to win this war they needed the ability to land armies and munitions and sustain them. This depended on the North Atlantic convoy system to a great extent. When you consider how the U.K. was on the brink of disaster in September 1942, then in November that we were able to participate fully with the Americans in the North African landings and be on the road to victory, seems incredible. To return to the shipping shortage, in the middle of June 1942, the U.S. war shipping administration in Washington and the British Ministry of War Transport held discussions to consider vessels suitable for requisitioning. The Allies at this time had their priorities on cargo ships which could bring war materials to the U.K. time and time again. This was not to be, and discussions centred on procuring American commercial vessels. Most of these vessels would have had to be withdrawn from their east coast passenger and goods role due to enemy danger and the difficulty of escorting or protecting them. It was considered at that time that some of these steam vessels could play a role in an invasion plan of Europe as troop carriers, hospital or accommodation ships. However, 11 ships were selected and after heavy boarding up, strengthening, and arming, only eight were considered suitable to cross the Atlantic. Most of the structural work was carried out at Baltimore.

Now came the problem of manning these 11 now British ships, flying the red duster. At the request of the British Authorities, the large shipping company, Coast Lines Ltd, Liverpool, under the chairmanship of Sir Alfred Read accepted the manning. The company's chief marine superintendent, Commander R.T. Park O.B.E., R.D. R.N.R. personally visited the U.S. and was responsible for deciding that the ships, as far as his considerable knowledge and experience were concerned, would be suitable to cross the Atlantic. The crews, 550 officers and men, all volunteers and on increased pay, sailed over to New York on the *Queen Mary*, and then on to Baltimore and finally to an adventure in which no one had a clue what would happen.

So, now come some questions, which will probably never be answered. Wars are a very nasty business, decisions and actions being continuously changed. The loss of lives and possible advantages are considered. Strict secrecy must be maintained at all times. The fewer people who know of the plans and decisions, the better. Actual vital decisions may never go beyond a spoken order and never appear in print. Clandestine operations, decoys, false information, traps etc, are all part of an operation to gain an advantage.

Look again at Convoy "Maniac"! The most critical period in which to cross the Atlantic. The ships carried no cargo, and were manned by volunteers. The escort was two of the oldest destroyers in the Royal Navy, completely unable to steam at high speeds, carry out continuous attacks on U-boats, stop to rescue survivors, rush back to catch up a convoy well dispersed, and shepherd them together, and with barely enough fuel to make a normal crossing. What possible vital role could these boarded up ships play in the U.K. at this time? In fact most of them had no important role, being laid up in rivers for months and months, some as accommodation or training facilities. Only after the invasion of Europe, when the safety of the Channel ports was ensured, would a few be used as troop carriers or hospital facilities. Some would never return to the U.S. but were sold on to Asia and other foreign countries.

What did the Convoy accomplish? The facts that cannot be disputed are that this small convoy of eight ships, river-boats, pleasure ships, all completely unsuitable to cross the Atlantic and never designed to, were heavily boarded and whale-backed with timber to protect the open spaces from the treacherous seas, some carrying extra fuel in drums on deck and fitted for action with some armament. There was no doubt that they were going to be attacked by U-boats in force. They had been sighted and reported to the German U-boat command in France from day one and subsequently informed in over 30 signals from Washington of the U-boats positions. The course of the convoy was never changed.

The initial sightings made by the U-boats were of an important convoy of large troopships and that belief never changed. The German U-boat command immediately put into operation a plan to totally destroy the convoy. A total of 17 U-boats were involved in two groups. After battling through the first group, a second group, which was engaging convoy S.C.100, was diverted to attack R.B.1. On completion of these attacks by overwhelming U-boat strength, the U-boats were spread over large areas and had to withdraw from the area for refuelling from a "milch-cow". As far as Convoy "Maniac" was concerned, she no longer existed after they had outrun the second attack and scattered. Instead the Convoy masters decided to use their higher speeds and make a dash to the U.K. ports. Further destroyer and air cover was sent out to them.

Some of the post-war articles about Convoy R.B.1 ran as follows:

That Convoy "Maniac" was indeed a decoy convoy which invited destruction in the Atlantic to safeguard another great convoy of vessels laden with munitions of war which were desperately wanted during World War II.

The eight ships engaged in trading on the Great Lakes sailed in a convoy intended to decoy enemy U-boats away from another great munitions and troop convoy which set sail from America at the same time. The plan succeeded and the latter got through without loss.

"Radio Berlin" crowed that German submarines had torpedoed several ships 'of the *Queen Mary* Class' and specifically mentioned the big liners *Duchess of Bedford* and *Reina Del Pacifico*. The German broadcast concluded by announcing that the number of ships sunk in the attack remained unknown, because the defense had been "so fierce".

The gallantry of this convoy of small American overnight steamers did not go unnoticed by the British either. King George VI included the masters, chief engineers and fourteen other officers from the fleet in his next honors list. The prime minister Churchill wrote of the honorees: "I am charged to record His Majesty's high appreciation of the service rendered."

Did he know more of this heroic convoy, that no-one in authority has ever mentioned? We may never know. The downside of this story, beside the ships lost, was the high loss of human beings so tragically killed while carrying out their service to their country: a total of 302 lives.

4

Mr Thomas V. Cottam, 2nd Mate, SS Northland

During my researches on Convoy "Maniac", a letter came into my possession from another "I was there" member. It was from Mr Thomas V. Cottam who had served as the 2nd Mate on the SS *Northland*, and I take this opportunity to mention some of the interesting remarks he has made of his recollections. Mr Cottam was in his eighties at the time in 1996.

I am now turned eighty but my recollection of the incidents concerning Convoy R.B.1 are very fresh in my mind. We sailed from St. John's, Newfoundland a.m. on the 21st September 1942 and during the afternoon took up our convoy station and I believe had some sort of a gun drill. Sometime later we were put on a zig-zag course to diagram No 33.

It so happened that a U-boat wolf-pack were patrolling the approaches to St. John's but were not expecting anything to emerge at that time, so as we approached they seemed not to have been in position to launch a decisive attack. They did let loose a number of torpedoes but missed, partly I suppose because they overestimated our draught. I took over the 12–4 p.m. watch at noon 22nd September and was concerned about the enormous error in the compass, Captain Becket having given me the ship's noon position. As the sun was shining for the first time since leaving Baltimore I was determined to get an azimuth. Mounting the ladder up to the bearing compass, over my shoulder I noticed a hoist of flags going up from the Commodore's ship the *Boston*. I made my way down to read the hoist through the ships' telescope. With the flags in focus, suddenly they all disappeared and in their place was a great column of smoke and flame and then I heard an almighty explosion. The torpedo had struck on the port side just under

28

the bridge. I doubt if anybody on the bridge could have survived.

We turned away hard to starboard but the steering gear broke down and we spent the next 2 to 3 hours steaming round and round in a circle. As we turned I saw the *Boston* settling down by the stern and within a very few minutes she had disappeared. I noticed two life boats leave the ship's side, one made for a ship following in the convoy, the other made for the destroyer which was about a mile away on the port quarter. After getting our steering gear back to work we raced full speed after the convoy which by this time was disappearing over the horizon. In so doing we had a far from healthy encounter with a U-boat on the surface. It was quite dark when we finally caught up with the rest, they were still on zig-zag courses so stood off to ascertain a suitable spot where we could join in. Very dangerous to get mixed up with ships steering in all directions. Finally I called up the Vice Commodore, SS *New York* to confirm the diagram. It was now so dark that I had to use a blue torch to make the signal. The reply came back on an aldis lamp that lit up the scene for miles.

The diagram was the same as previously but we discovered we had joined the convoy on the wrong leg. The Vice Commodore should have been on our port bow but now turned up on the starboard bow. Captain Beckett decided to stop everything. At that moment with the Vice Commodore SS *New York* fairly close on the starboard bow I saw a blinding flash and blast in almost the exact place where the Commodore's ship SS *Boston* had been struck. There were two or three further explosions out on our starboard side and one almighty explosion and fire we took to come from the direction of our destroyer escort. At this point the chief engineer hove into the wheel-house and demanded if we were going to remain like a sitting duck and be blown out of the water. Captain Beckett said, 'Give me the steam and we'll make a run for it.' Anyhow we had the steam, which was never in doubt and after doing a bit of dodging and ducking arrived safely in Londonderry.

The German side of the story indicates that at the time they certainly believed that we were a troop-carrying convoy; so important in fact that after we had broken through the first patrol, less the *Boston* and *New York*, they called in a second pack that was operating to the north to intercept us, which they did on 24/25th. It always seemed to me that there was a delicate leakage of information and at the same time cover up, to make the R.B.1 something other than what it really was. There was a rumour that the real convoy was further to the south.

5

Honours, Awards and Decorations

Convoy R.B.1 September 1942
Merchant ships manned by Coast Lines Ltd., Liverpool.

SS *Boston*	R.S.C. Young	Master (Posthumous) Commended for courage and devotion to duty.	
SS *New York*	C. Mayers	Master (Posthumous) Commended for courage and devotion to duty.	
SS *Yorktown*	W.P. Boylan	Master	OBE.
	E. Toolan	Chief Engineer	OBE.
	D. Mclachlan	Chief Radio Officer (Posthumous) Commended for courage and devotion to duty.	
	H.O. Papworth	Chief Officer Commended for good service.	
	C. Winter	Second Radio Officer Commended for good service.	
	A. Budden	Third Radio Officer Commended for good service.	
SS *Northland*	J. Beckett	Master Commended for good service.	
	J. Firth	Chief Engineer	OBE.
	Mr Humphreys	Chief Radio Officer Commended for good service.	

SS *Southland*	J. Willians	Master	OBE.
	J. F. Jack	Chief Engineer	OBE.
SS *President Warfield*	J.R. Williams	Master	OBE.
	J.S. Penwill	Chief Engineer	OBE.
SS *New Bedford*	R. Hardy	Master	OBE. MBE.
	J. Anderson	Chief Engineer	OBE.
	H.W.F. Kaye	Chief Officer (Posthumous) Commended for courage and devotion to duty.	
SS *Naushon*	J.J. Murray	Master Commended for good service.	
	J.H. Harrison	Chief Engineer	OBE.

6

The Merchant Navy

Undoubtedly the service that contributed so much towards maintaining a standard of life in Britain and giving her the ability to continue the war to a final victory, was the Merchant Navy. These men, who chose to crew merchant ships whatever their destinations, sizes or cargoes all around the world in appalling weather and tough conditions and always very vulnerable to enemy action, should have received the nation's highest praise, but they rarely did so. Some men who had been through terrible conditions as survivors returned again and again, and many only to lose their lives. In spite of the vast amount of books and literature produced about World War II, it still seems far too difficult to visualise these great convoys in the North Atlantic and Arctic, without far more records of the experiences of the ships' officers and men.

The Battle of the Atlantic, which this story is mainly about, saw enormous destruction of merchant shipping and hundreds of thousands of tons of vital food and war supplies, and the tragic loss of thousands of lives. The lives lost by the Merchant Navy in the North Atlantic reached over 50,000 dead, about 31,000 manning British ships. Ten of our Allied countries lost about 19,000 between them. To these figures must be added those men from neutral countries who had volunteered to join the Allies, and not a few from Ireland. The D.E.M.S. – Defensively Equipped Merchant Ships – consisting of Royal Navy gunners and Royal Army Maritime Regiment gunners, lost over 4,000 men. No figures can account for the thousands of seamen who were injured or suffered forever from their experiences.

The merchant shipping losses started from day one on the commencement of World War II on September 3rd 1939. In the last four months of 1939, 220 ships were sunk totalling over 750,000 tons, in the Atlantic. In the first nine months of the war, shipping losses were mostly confined to the Atlantic Ocean and it was after June 1940 when the losses started in the Mediterranean and other theatres. For the year of 1940, just over 1,000 ships and over 3.6 million tons were lost in the Atlantic and 1941 continued with over 870 ships and over 3.3 million tons lost. 1942 was to be the year when shipping was at its most critical state with almost 1,200 ships sunk and over 6.1 million tons lost. In 1943 the losses thankfully reduced to just over 360 ships and over 2.1 million tons, and 1944 showed almost 120 ships sunk and over 0.5 million tons lost. 1945 was to see an end to the five and a half years of carnage, and peace for this vast Atlantic grave of ships and men. Ships sunk that year totalled 91 and just over 370,000 tons lost. The total losses of merchant shipping in the Atlantic Ocean vary slightly from different sources, but it would not be too far out to say that between 3,800 and 3,900 ships were sunk and well over 17 million tons lost. Ships lost in the North Atlantic alone account for between 80 and 90% of the total Atlantic losses.

In 1942 the ships and supplies being convoyed from America and Canada to Britain were most vulnerable. The U-boats up to 1942 had been very successful in their campaign further south in the Atlantic with ships sailing from the American and West Indies and also Africa and East Indies. It would be some time before the convoy system was introduced to an efficient state on the east coast of America, bringing an end to the U-boats' "Happy Time". Once the convoy system started with more escorts and air patrols, the U-boats became very vulnerable and faced more and more losses. Doenitz decided to withdraw these groups and return them to the North Atlantic. The following figures show just how successful was this decision on the North Atlantic convoys of 1942.

Convoy Losses in 1942

Month	Ships Lost	Tonnage to Nearest 1,000
January	48	277
February	73	430
March	95	534
April	60	391
May	120	576
June	124	623
July	98	487
August	96	508
September	95	474
October	62	400
November	83	509
December	46	262
Total	1006	5,471,000 Tons

In 1942 the total Atlantic losses were 1,170 ships and in the North Atlantic alone 1,006 ships or 86%. The total global losses, all theatres, were 1,664 ships, giving the North Atlantic about 60%.

In 1942, with these enormous losses of ships and supplies, it was becoming a very close call whether Britain could survive. Some reports have mentioned that food stocks in Britain had gone below a three month supply with a tighter squeeze on food rationing and the oil fuel position becoming more acute as oil tankers became a key target for the "Wolf packs". But one of the most remarkable feats that was accomplished towards the end of 1942 was the successful landings in North Africa and a reversal for our land forces, giving them the initiative for further victories. There is no doubt that in 1942 the ships that had battled against heavy odds to bring the vital supplies to our shores had provided a mass of war equipment and thousands of fighting men for the assault.

It must not be forgotten what the North Atlantic troopship movements had achieved in 1942 and 1943. Convoys of these liners rarely exceeded four ships and the "monster liners" sailed singly. Their very high speed exceeded the endurance of the escorts and any escorting was only possible by ships meeting en route and then being left astern. In 1942 over 226,000 Allied fighting men arrived in Britain, and in 1943 the total was more than 681,000.

The *Queen Mary* and *Queen Elizabeth* carried out about 15,000 troops each. *Aquitania* and *Mauritania* carried about 8,000 troops each, with *Pasteur, Empress of Scotland* and *Andes* carrying about 4,500 troops each. These "monster liners", crossing the Atlantic both ways, also carried back to America Allied servicemen; in 1942 almost 59,000 men and in 1943, 127,000 men. Their movements in every aspect had to be highly secret and many seamen engaged in Atlantic convoying never saw them from first to last.

Over 75,000 ships sailed in escorted convoys during World War II and over 225,000 crew served in British registered ships. About 175 Naval vessels were lost in the North Atlantic and many thousands of lives. The convoys to North Russia, which was a continuation from the North Atlantic, lost over 100 merchant ships and 19 warships, with tragic loss of life in terrible weather conditions of almost 900 seamen and 2,000 officers and men of the Royal Navy. There were at least 21 commodores of Atlantic convoys who lost their lives and ships.

7

V & W Class Destroyers

When I joined the Royal Navy as a boy 2nd Class at the ripe old age of 15 years, in the middle of 1937, it was a navy that consisted mainly of a regular force of all volunteers, who had signed on for The King's Shilling for the first period of their active service. This first period was for 12 years starting at the age of 18. With the Navy's infinite wisdom, this enabled hundreds of young boys to be trained and drafted to warships for service home and abroad, with the added distinction that for about three years their service would not be counted towards a pension. On completion of the 12 years' service, men could volunteer for a further 10 years giving them a pension after 22 years service. This would be subject to recommendation from senior officers and their service records. This system with some variations was how the pre-war Royal Navy operated as far as the lower deck was concerned. So with boys and junior ratings joining their first warships or subsequent draftings, their new companions would be men who had seen many years of sea experience on all types of warships serving on many foreign stations that the British Empire protected. In 1937, the armistice of the Great War was only 19 years in the past, so there were quite a few veterans still serving their time for a pension. Little did they realise that events leading to a world conflict would prevent them leaving the service and would extend their active service to 1945 at least.

You may ask, what has all this to do with V & W destroyers? Those who have had some experience of matelot's yarns will be aware that they last some time, often digress and even forget what the subject was in the first place, especially if told after "tot" time. However it was these old sea dogs who instilled in us 'sprogs', as we were referred to, the main ingredients of becoming a real sailor, one of which was that you served in the "Boats", i.e. destroyers. The greatest accolade was to have served in V & W destroyers in a raging "hooligan" (gale), and this would be an experience that would never be forgotten.

It would seem, without doubt, that prior to the Great War, naval design of warships was revolutionised by the British with the introduction of the new battleship HMS *Dreadnought*. This new design made all the existing battleships of all the world powers obsolete at a stroke and gave the Royal Navy an advantage of several years. Over the years this design was copied in many respects and built upon by most world powers. However, by the start of the 1914–1918 war, there were some old destroyers and others which really needed modernising to carry out a wartime role. Although every effort was being made to increase the numbers of destroyers, the Germans were also designing destroyers which were to be more modern and with better armaments than the British.

Not to be left behind in this vital armament race, the Admiralty design team, and no doubt the ship builders, produced a design that would once again give the Royal Navy a fighting edge for some years to come. This was to be a series of ships that were to have names starting with a V and others with a W. Quite soon it was accepted as the V & W Class. These warships were designed during the early years of the 1914–1918 war and the war emergency programme ordered 25 initially, followed by a further 25 with smaller orders to follow, the first orders being placed in 1916. At first it was thought that the first five ships completed would become destroyer flotilla leaders, but this was cancelled and all this class was kept for destroyer duties. A larger design had to be produced to act as the leaders. These destroyers were quite impressive at that time and the leaders were still, prior to 1939, some of the most powerful destroyers in service in the world. Although several V & W destroyers were completed in 1917 and 1918 and carried out wartime duties with very high success and efficiency, the full value and potential of these "Boats" working in flotillas or independently was never to be known, as the armistice of November 11th 1918 ceased all hostilities.

It was to be 21 years later, when World War II began, that the qualities and enormous potential of the now "old" V & Ws were tested, and certainly not found lacking, whatever was asked of them.

To visualise what made these destroyers tick it may assist the reader to know a little of the design first, and a brief history of the class.

The V & W Class Destroyers

V & W destroyers could always be recognised in profile, mostly by their funnels of different heights and diameters. Some had the taller thinner funnel forward and the shorter thicker one aft, while other ships had them in reverse. Even with later modifications when one funnel was removed they could still be picked out easily.

The earliest Vs and Ws:

1100 tons and up to 1500 tons deep load

300 feet in length and 30 feet in the beam

3 boilers, all geared turbines, 2 shafts

Fuel oil 320 to 360 tons

Feed water 20 tons

Drinking and food 7 tons

Designed ship horse power 27,000

Producing speeds, subject to load draughts, of 30 to 34 knots.

Armament:

4 single 4" Mark V guns

2 single, 2 PDR pom-poms

Machine and Lewis guns

Five 21 inch torpedo tubes in one triple (forward) and one double (aft) mountings situated abaft the after funnel.

Complement:

134 officers and men

Some of these destroyers were equipped for mine laying and had rails fitted for releasing the mines over the stern.

The total number of V & W Class destroyers built was 68, of which 52 were completed during 1917 and 1918, and 16 were completed during 1919 to 1924. By the start of World War II the number of V & Ws in service was 58, the losses of 10 destroyers being as follows:

1918
Wallace.
1919
Vehement, Verulam and *Vittoria* : lost in the Baltic.
1932
Valhalla : scrapped.
1936
Valkyrie, Vectic, Venturous and *Violent* : handed over to the breakers as part payment to retain SS *Majestic.*
1938
Walrus : wrecked and scrapped.

Also pre World War II, *Vendetta, Vampire, Waterhen* and *Voyager* were transferred to the Royal Australian Navy.

By 1939 many of this class had been allocated to a number of groups for modifications and conversions, some with heavier armament and boiler room conversions enabling more fuel space and so on. The detail of the ships involved is best left to the naval historians, but generally the fates of the 58 destroyers in service at the start of World War II were:

Start of WWII	Lost during WWII
10 Unaltered	9
15 Modified as Fast Escort vessels	4
11 Modified as Short Range Escort Vessels	4
22 Modified as Long Range Escort Vessels	2
58	19

During the period between the two World Wars, international

policies and agreements limited the number of warships being built and also their size and tonnage. It also meant that many warships were to be laid up or scrapped in accordance with ratios set between the naval powers. The British stuck to the agreements, resulting in many ships going to the breakers' yards and many destroyers finishing up on "Rotten Row", hauled up on the mud flats, berthed side by side, and virtually left to rot. Other foreign naval powers were rather more cautious of applying the agreements, and continued to build and retain warships in defiance, both in numbers and tonnage. This position of dishonesty was well known by all the naval powers at least by the mid 1930s, and it may be due to the Admiralty's recognition of this that quite a few destroyers were saved and brought back into an active role. With the lessons learned from the convoy experiences of the Great War, it was realised that Britain was very dangerously short of destroyers to carry out fleet duties, convoy escorts and many other duties.

By the time of the Munich crisis in late 1938, and the mobilisation of the reserve fleet, the strength and weaknesses of British naval power had become apparent. Every attempt had to be made to build up the Navy's strength after the period of enforced neglect, but nothing could disguise the fact that our destroyer and escort numbers and strength were pitifully low, and that if a war was to break out in the near future, then the Royal Navy was to have a scrap on their hands for some years to come.

By the start of World War II, the 58 remaining V & W Class destroyers were ready, together with all the later and more modern classes for the wartime duties. The Norwegian Campaign was to be the first of the large naval operations of World War II in which the destroyers showed their versatility in surface actions, mining, landing troops and equipment, evacuation of troops and many more vital duties. Some would say that their finest hour was the evacuation of Dunkirk and off the coasts of Holland, Belgium and France in 1940. In Operation "Dynamo" a total of 56 destroyers participated, lifting out almost 103,000 troops of about 338,000 saved. 28 V

41

& Ws were included and 4 sunk; *Valentine, Whitley, Wessex* and *Wakeful*. Many sustained damage and casualties. 40 destroyers earned themselves the right to wear the battle honour "Dunkirk 1940".

V & W Class Destroyer Losses 1939–1945

1940 7 Ships Lost

D49	*Valentine*	15.5.1940	Bombed
D23	*Whitley*	19.5.1940	Bombed
D43	*Wessex*	24.5.1940	Bombed
D88	*Wakeful*	29.5.1940	E-boat
D30	*Whirlwind*	5.7.1940	U-34 torpedoed
D88	*Wren*	27.7.1940	Bombed
D53	*Venetia*	9.10.1940	Mined

1941 2 Ships Lost

D21	*Wryneck*	27.4.1941	Bombed
D22	*Waterhen* R.A.N.	30.6.1941	Bombed

1942 6 Ships Lost

D23	*Vimiera*	9.1.1942	Mined
D37	*Vortigern*	15.3.1942	E-boat
D68	*Vampire* R.A.N.	23.9.1942	Bombed – Japanese
D62	*Wildswan*	17.6.1942	Bombed
D31	*Voyager* R.A.N.	23.9.1942	Bombed – Japanese
D72	*Veteran*	26.9.1942	U-404 torpedoed (Convoy R.B.1)

1943–1944 3 Ships Lost

D96	*Worcester*	23.12.1943	Mined
D25	*Warwick*	20.2.1944	U-413 torpedoed
D35	*Wrestler*	6.6.1944	Mined

1945 1 Ship Lost

D41	*Walpole*	6.1.1945	Mined

Losses caused by

U-Boats	3
E-Boats	2
Bombing	9
Mines	5
Total	19

A total of 39 V & W class destroyers survived World War II. Almost every ship had sustained damage by enemy action, the ramming of U-boats and the atrocious weather they had to endure over six years. Many were patched up and repaired on several occasions. They had participated in all theatres of war and during their lifetime had steamed about one quarter to half a million miles.

The survivors

Vendetta R.A.N.	*Vesper*	*Wolsey*	*Valorous*
Versatile	*Woolston*	*Vanity*	*Vidette*
Windsor	*Vega*	*Vivacious*	*Vivien*
Verdun	*Viscount*	*Witherington*	*Vivien*
Walker	*Wivern*	*Viceroy*	*Winchester*
Watchman	*Westminster*	*Wolfhound*	*Westcott*
Winchelsea	*Vansittart*	*Venomous*	*Verity*
Wolverine	*Wishart*	*Witch*	*Vimy*
Vanessa	*Vanquisher*	*Velox*	*Vanoc(Convoy R.B.1)*
Volunteer	*Wanderer*	*Whitehall*	

By 1949 none of these ships which had paid such a high price and given so much in the war at sea remained. They had all been sold and broken up for scrap. It seems tragic and unbelievable that a nation which prided itself on its maritime history could not save just one V & W destroyer for the British heritage. For the war veterans and the generations that followed it would serve as a reminder of what conditions were like in this war at sea for days, months and years on end.

In the war at sea, a war of attrition with the U-boat

menace, destroyers, corvettes and escort vessels had a far more difficult task than to attack the U-boats. The primary duties of the escorts was to protect the ships of the convoys, to enable the vital lifeline of food, fuel, supplies and war materials to arrive safely in British ports. Without this lifeline Britain would have been brought to its knees. With the size of the escort ships, destroyers, corvettes and others, one of the main problems was the amount of fuel that could be carried and the rate of consumption during the crossing. The escorts always covered more miles at different speeds, to shepherd the ships and stragglers. Also, in cases of ships being sunk they assisted with rescue work and if possible located and attacked any U-boat's position. It is quite remarkable that with the limited scope of time and fuel the escorts contributed to so many U-boat killings. The V & Ws and their leaders contributed to the destruction of 38 German U-boats and 6 Italian submarines. Some of these successes were accomplished by individual operations and many more by "J.E.", joint attacks with other escorts, and "J.A.", joint aircraft, as follows:

U-boats Destroyed by the V & Ws

U 55	*Whitshed* J.E. + J.A.	U 357	*Vanessa* J.E.
U 69	*Viscount*	U 360	Keppel Ldr J.E.
U 70	*Wolverine*	U 390	*Wanderer* J.E.
U 74	*Wishart. Wrestler* J.A.	U 392	*Vanoc* J.E. + J.A.
U 76	*Wolverine* J.E.	U 394	Keppel. *Whitehall* J.E. + J.A.
U 99	*Walker*	U 401	*Wanderer* J.E.
U 100	*Vanoc. Walker*	U 411	*Wrestler*
U 125	*Vidette*	U 413	*Vidette* J.E.
U 147	*Wanderer* J.E.	U 581	*Westcott*
U 162	*Vimy* J.E.	U 587	*Volunteer* J.E.
U 187	*Vimy* J.E.	U 661	*Viscount*
U 207	*Veteran* J.E.	~~U 651~~	~~*Violet* J.E.~~
U 274	*Vidette* J.E. + J.A.	U 713	Keppel Ldr
U 282	*Vidette* J.E.	U 714	*Wivern* J.E.
U 305	*Wanderer* J.E.	U 732	Douglas Ldr
U 306	*Whitehall* J.E.	U 761	*Wishart* J.E. + J.A.

U 314	*Whitehall* J.E.	U 878	*Vanquisher* J.E.
U 340	*Witherington* J.E. + J.A.	U 1195	*Watchman*
U 354	Keppel Ldr J.E.	U 1274	*Viceroy*

The six Italian submarines were the *Gondar, Durbo, Glauco, Alessandro, Malaspina* and *Dagabur*. The *Vanessa* had the unique distinction of sinking a German submarine in World War I and World War II; 27.7.1918, UB 107 and 26.12.1942 U-357.

8

A Sailor's Life On Board a V & W

It would really be presumptuous to describe the life on board these ships without having personally experienced it. Some very good authors have described in various books and articles the life and conditions that had to be endured at sea. Perhaps the best accounts come from the escorting of North Atlantic convoys and those engaged in the Arctic conditions.

My drafting to HMS *Vanoc* in 1941 can only be described as a mental shock. I had joined the *Andrew* (Royal Navy) in 1937 and had served in HMS *Iron Duke*, Jellicoe's flagship at Jutland, with the exalted rank of Boy 1st Class. My next ship was an almost new 6 inch 'Town Class' cruiser, HMS *Glasgow* which was to be my home for nearly three years – peace and war time. One of the main objectives of this ship was to be the pride of the fleet in gunnery, armaments and seamanship. This was a real "pusser" ship, spotless in its exterior painting and armaments and between decks. Uniform and correct dress was always rigidly adhered to. It was impossible for any crew member not to be proud to serve on this ship.

So, here I was, now a Leading Seaman – gunnery trained, standing on a filthy overcrowded jetty, dressed so smartly that I would pass for a King's parade, gazing with a stunned expression at this apparition in front of me. She was laid alongside a jetty in the Gladstone docks at Liverpool with several more destroyers. All these ships wore the look that showed they had endured the worst the sea could offer. Work was being carried out on the ships by the "dockies", and stores and supplies were being replenished. As far as dress was concerned, there did not seem much distinction between the

46

dockyard workers and the ship's crew, except perhaps the dockies were smarter. Deciding to enter the lion's den, I picked up my steaming bag which contained only essential kit. My main kitbag and full kit for touring the globe including tropical gear and pith helmet was left behind in the "safety" of the stores at Portsmouth barracks. Like many similar matelots, our surplus kit was so secure that it was never seen again. With a well lashed hammock containing a horse-hair mattress, one blanket and other articles of kit that wouldn't go in the steaming bag, I crossed the plank onto the ship and gave a smart salute. This act of courtesy to the old girl was greeted by several matelots in disguise, or as I soon found out, normal dress, with "look lads, a real sailor". All I can say is that they must have taken some warped liking to me and given me preferential treatment instead of the normal accidental christening with a bucket of slops. After the formalities of joining the ship were over, and my new mess mates were making an urn of tea, about 1600 hours, I was gleefully told that we would be casting off at 1800 hours to escort another Atlantic convoy, after being in dock for less than 48 hours.

So for me, the transformation from being a pusser sailor to my new shipmates' sea dress and attitudes came remarkably quickly, with less flannel and a pleasant comfortable feeling with all the new shipmates. This was not too difficult as the complement was only about 130 or so, but even this would be increased soon to unbelievable overcrowding.

Serving on destroyers could not have been more vastly different from serving on the capital ships. Almost every aspect was different. With V & Ws the first thing you were bound to notice was the shortage of space. Everywhere was cramped and made compact. There were no lockers to hang up and store clothes, but compartments under the mess deck seats nearest the ship's side which had to be shared by all those in the mess. Everything had to be folded up, sometimes the shoregoing clothes wrapped in canvas or paper, but there was always dampness and mildew to contend with. Hammocks were stored and packed vertically in netting to save space. Metal rails and hooks were part of the fitments to sling your hammock in your mess or flat. But these positions had their regular established users and there were far too few for everyone to be able to sling a hammock, so those others had to sleep on the mess tables, mess seating and on the decks. In the two years and more I served on the V & Ws the only times I could sling a hammock was if some of the crew were on overnight leave. The other times I either sat hunched up or on the deck, and many sailors were in the same position as myself. Hammocks that were slung were so tight together that they moved and rolled as one unit. During convoy duties those men coming off watch would take off their duffel coats, oilskins, rubber boots, scarves, balaclava, etc and turn in fully dressed. There were very few, if any, times that normal clothing could be removed, and for those sleeping rough practically all clothes stayed put. Those V & Ws like the *Vanoc* were unaltered from the time of their completion in 1917 and 1918, and for many it would be years before the opportunity came for modernisation. For HMS *Vanoc* it was to be April/November 1943 at Thorney-crofts, Southampton.

Ventilation, heating and insulation in the living spaces were so inefficient as to be non-existent. The seamen's mess-decks were situated directly under the forecastle deck, one mess being poked into the pointed section and shared with a paint and rope locker. There was one mess each side in the wider section. Between these three messes was situated the "Donkey" steam engine for driving the capstan and working the ship's cables. This was an area that created its own grease, oil and steam environment, but it had its advantage when the mess-decks were so cold that even a crack of steam to the engine gave some relief. This secret manoeuvre was often discovered and shut off. After all steam was for driving the ship – nothing else.

The stokers, signalmen and other specialised rates had their mess-decks one deck lower, with access and escape by one round manhole hatch and steel ladder. The awkwardness of men having to come up and down sometimes at speed, bringing down hot food and drinks, returning with washing up water and gash and so on seems unbelievable. Also the hatch cover had to be clipped shut at sea, producing a watertight compartment, so that making the cover continuously open and shut, unclipped and clipped up again from either side just magnified the problem. It was rarely, if ever, mentioned that if the ship was damaged, requiring a rapid evacuation, it would be extremely difficult to escape from. With all ships, the battening down of hatches to living spaces, and single or too few escape points, are dangers and perhaps none greater than in the smaller and older ships. The other quarters for the officers and non-commissioned officers were just as bleak, overcrowded and with minimal facilities. Generally speaking for the V & Ws, we were all in it together.

A further problem was that there were no facilities to dry clothing. There was little or no shelter on the upper decks, the bridge was open to the elements, so bridge personnel, gunners, depth charge and torpedo tube crews, and others stood a very high chance of being soaked continuously from the treacherous sea. After changing watches the outside clothing was hung up to dry but was invariably just as wet when required for the next watch. The chief stoker allowed some clothes lines to be strung where safe in the boiler room, to assist drying out, but it was not enough when the weather was at its most severe. As mentioned, other clothing was rarely removed or washed until the ships returned for fuelling, stores, provisions and so on, and even then, if the boilers had to be blown down for cleaning, it was a case of using any dockyard washing and toilet facilities.

It was no problem to eat the food if you had a cast iron stomach, but most of the crews, who were only normal, were affected by the terrible weather at times, the violent rolling, tossing and turning of the ship, one moment riding the top of the waves and the next plunging down into a deep trough with a great crash and an unimaginable shudder throughout the whole structure. These conditions could last for days and weeks, especially during the long winters in the North Atlantic and Arctic. It was surprising how even the men who were unfortunately always prone to sea-sickness could quickly recover their stability and appetite once the weather subsided.

The victualling, cooking, preparing and serving the food on these ships was really something to remember. Until the early 1920s the ships' arrangements were referred to as "general messing", where all the food came from the ship's stores, was mostly prepared and cooked by the ship's cooks and collected from the ship's galley by the mess's representative, the "cook of the rook". This was a duty everyone took turns at, together with the washing up and keeping the mess clean. The menu was the same for everyone. After this period the system of "canteen messing" was introduced. Each man was credited with an allowance for his daily food, which was calculated from a total for the number of men in that mess. The ship's stores, under the command of "Jack Dusty", consisted of mostly non-perishable items such as tea, sugar, condensed milk, tins of meats, etc. Also for a short period after leaving port there could be other perishable items available, such as bread, fresh fruit, and eggs. It must be remembered that these ships had no form of refrigeration whatever, so that the perishables had a short "shelf life". The fresh meat which had come aboard (that is carried not walked on) was stored on deck in what was loosely known as the meat safe, which was a metal box screwed just above the deck with a wire mesh door, similar to a rabbit's hutch, with a padlock, often changed as the key got lost, and a loose canvas flap. The issue of this meat would normally be made before 0900 daily. "Jack Dusty" with his pencil and pad would take station at the meat safe, with the wooden chopping block, cleaver, saw and carving knife at the ready. A set of hanging scales would be hooked overhead and the "cook of the rook" from each mess would appear by magic and call out the mess number. Jack Dusty looking at his pad would call out the weight allocated to that mess and his assistant, an able seaman, whose butchery skills were yet to surface, hacked off the required amount. By a clever and ingenious method the bone in the meat was included in the weight, causing some ribald comments to those receiving the issue. After the issue the tools of the trade were stowed away and the safe locked. This enabled the meat to continue its process of being bashed about from side to side and regularly washed

50

down when the decks were awash until, having passed many colour changes, it was eventually cooked or ditched.

The other advantage of "canteen messing" was that on board there was a canteen manager, a N.A.A.F.I. employee who had a small cupboard for storing and supplying food and items of general use. His canteen was so small that only he had space to stand inside, customers using a hatch. The canteen manager would go ashore to the N.A.A.F.I. stores or shops and purchase all his requirements. Some of the food would be sides of bacon and perishable items. He had an astute brain, which did not leave him holding goods that could not last or be disposed of. These canteens and N.A.A.F.I. staffs carried out excellent and efficient work throughout World War II in places of extreme danger, and many lost their lives. Not enough praise was ever given to them.

To purchase goods from the canteen was done in two ways, one by persons paying cash for their own use, and the second by a mess purchasing bacon, eggs, bread, cakes, biscuits etc. for meals. These purchases, all duly signed for, would come from the men's allowance. It did not take too long to discover the rudimentary rule of good housekeeping at the end of each month, which was that stores purchased from the ship's stores plus goods purchased from the canteen should equal the mess's allowance. There was more often than not an imbalance on the wrong side, resulting in digging into the money belt. Each month was balanced either by paying up or, most unusually, sharing out any surplus.

Before advancing to the cooking stage, one advantage of canteen messing was that within the limits of availability and cooking utensils it was possible for the different messes to have different dinner (main meal) menus. All the meals were obtained and prepared by the duty "cook of the rook" of each mess. This would involve peeling spuds and fresh vegetables and (in those couple of days after sailing) opening the cans of peas, beans, sausages, meat and so on, mutilating further the meat from the meat safe, and making pastry for "clacker". With everyone taking a turn there were some weird and wonderful results, and also names. Possible the favourite

51

dinner (midday) was "pot mess" especially on cold days. This started with a large cast-iron pot and finished full up with anything available that resembled food – meat, peas, beans, oxo's, spuds etc. Another meal would be "straight rush". This started with a large dish and finished loaded with a joint of meat surrounded by potatoes. Other messes would decide how to use the available victuals, not forgetting "toad in the hole".

The main meal of the day was undoubtedly the midday dinner and with the aperitif of "Nelson's blood", you were ready to eat a horse, which may have been the case. Any meal time was always dictated by events happening at that time, be it the weather or someone out there trying to sink you. Sometimes you would just have to eat what was possible and when. Even the rum issue scheduled for 1100 hours, and neat at that, was delayed some hours but to my knowledge never abandoned. In general the men's meals consisted of:

Breakfast – Mug of tea and a fag or your purchase from the canteen.
Dinner – Big eats.
Tea-time – Mug of tea, bread if available, possible something from the canteen.
Supper – Mug of tea and two fags, anything you could scrounge.

Now for the "Jewel in the Crown", the galley. This was situated amidships just below the break from the forecastle deck and was a compartment with side doors about 10 feet by 6 feet. Across the long side was installed the galley stove and bunker. This was a large black kitchen stove with several ovens and top hobs. It was coal-burning and the whole galley and contents were commanded by a Petty Officer cook, just one aboard. Needless to say his duties were to cook all the variety of dishes brought to his galley by 0900 daily and those from the officer's steward. This was also the only place on the ship where you could obtain drinking water, boiled or cold. The cook needed to be a jigsaw expert to position and reposition all the pots, pans and oven dishes on his stove and also to have them ready for collecting at midday. Sometimes it would be impossible to have open pans boiling away when the weather was at its worst so changes were made. There was always a large pot of "Kie" (cocoa), hot on the stove, ready for men sent down from the bridge, guns etc. to take a can back to the duty men. This cocoa was made from large slabs broken up and boiled with added brown sugar and condensed milk, usually forming a thick layer of fat on the top. I cannot imagine anyone these days wanting to drink this special nectar, but thousands of matelots were weaned on it.

Water provision was the demon of these ships, especially for domestic use and drinking. The storage was insufficient. There was one tank wingside for domestic use, washing and shaving, washing clothes, scrubbing messes etc, but this was not drinking water. In the old V & Ws this tank was often taken over to carry extra fuel to increase the range of the escorts. When this happened it was the end of domestic usage of water. This water tank when in use was operated from a hand pump on the main deck to buckets or to a steam kettle to heat up. The drinking water was always restricted. The capacity of this tank when full was only seven tons, just over 1,500 gallons, and this was for use in cooking food, hot and cold drinks for between the designed complement of 134 men to the 170 plus which would inevitably follow in the future, for periods of seven days or more depending on fuel consumption. The Petty Officer cook was held responsible for the conservation of this precious commodity and closed the supply valve for all but short periods at meal times. The galley had a small tank which again was filled by hand pump mostly for the kettle on the stove.

One vital factor of the galley which caused concern was the fact that it was coal-burning, with its own small smoke stack. The coal was carried on board in sacks and stored in a small bunker under the main deck with a watertight manhole. In the galley was a smaller bunker for daily use. Invariably the stocks of coal were saturated in water. it was always preferable to clear and remove the hot ashes and to bank up the fire during dark hours, but there were unavoidable times especially in daytime when the old girl decided to belch out a nice black smoke. This action was quickly followed by a raucous voice crying in the wind, "What bloody message are you sending to the U-boats", usually followed by a bucket of water dousing the fire for some time, probably until dark.

These V & W Class veterans of World War I, and later their counterparts the 50 U.S.A. destroyers handed over to Britain, were recognised as the worst of all naval ships and besides the reasons previously mentioned there were many others. The convoy escorts came from many of the Allied countries and were integrated into one force with ships old and new, modern, not so modern and ancient. Undoubtedly it was the old V & Ws and the 50 old American destroyers which Roosevelt had transferred to Britain to ease the severe shortage of escorts that had the worst time. The old V & Ws dating back to 1914 would have been made obsolete and scrapped in the early 1930s. Although some of the original designs had improved the sizes of armament, making some more powerful than others, they were all sister-ships. It was remarkable that it was not until 1942 that an investigation into the appalling conditions experienced in destroyers was carried out. The V & Ws from 1917 to 1920 were even then considered to be far below what normal conditions should be, and hence crews were paid "hard lying" money of a few coppers a day. As a result of this investigation into living conditions aboard, Admiralty fleet orders introduced better standards to improve those conditions.

These new standards seemed a drop in the ocean to the main problem and concerned with such items as insulation, heating and the covering of the bare exposed steel of the ship's side, bulkheads and overhead, most of these areas being cold and notorious for condensation. These improvements were to be made during dock repairs and when possible to do so, perhaps not for months or years. The new standard to "improve" conditions however was to reinstate the extra pay of "hard lying" money, which was to be one shilling and six pence per day. Even this concession, although most welcome, had an air of grudgingness about it, in that it would only be paid from

SS *President Warfield* (1928) (National Maritime Museum, London)

HMS *Vanoc* (National Maritime Museum, London)

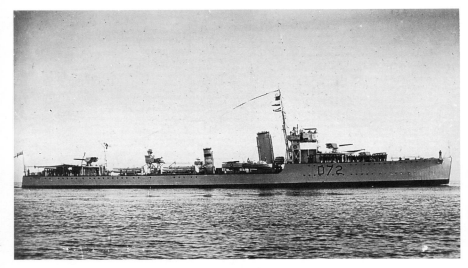

HMS *Veteran* (National Maritime Museum, London)

The *Boston* (National Maritime Museum, London)

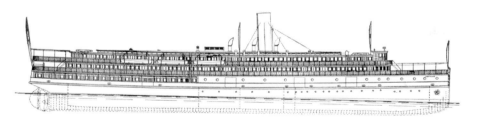

STEAMER
NORTHLAND
BUILT FOR THE
NORFOLK & WASHINGTON
STEAMBOAT CO.,
BY
HARLAN & HOLLINGSWORTH CORP'N
WILMINGTON, DEL.
1911

The *Northland* (National Maritime Museum, London)

SS *Derbyshire*, identified in error (National Maritime Museum, London)

SS *Viceroy of India*, identified in error (National Maritime Museum, London)

SS *Reina del Pacifico*, identified in error (National Maritime Museum, London)

R.M.S. *Queen Mary* in her wartime grey paint (National Maritime Museum, London)

Ray Freeman (left) and the
author at the service of
remembrance for HMS
Veteran, September 1992

Ray Freeman and the author,
who served on HMS *Vanoc*
in Convoy R.B.1. 'Maniac'

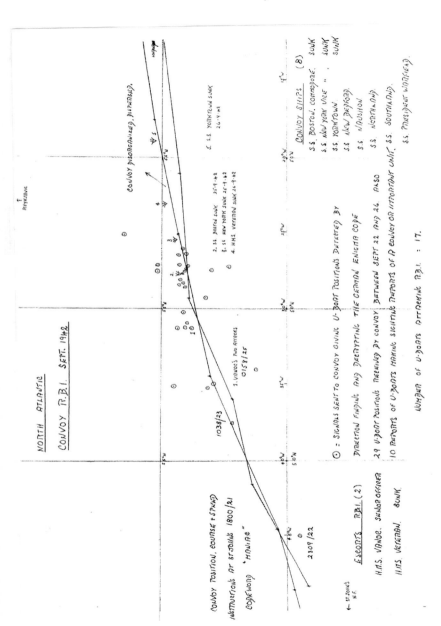

NORTH ATLANTIC

CONVOY R.B.1. SEPT. 1942

CONVOY POSITION, COURSE & SPEED

INSTRUCTIONS AT ST JOHNS 1800/21
CODEWORD "MAWIRE"

CONVOY DISORGANIZED, DISPERSED.

E.S.S. YORKTOWN SUNK 26-9-42

2. SS BOSTON SUNK 25-9-42
3. SS NEW YORK SUNK 25-9-42
4. H.M.S. VETERAN SUNK 26-9-42

1. U-BOATS TWO ATTACKS 0158/25

⊙ = SIGNALS SENT TO CONVOY GIVING U-BOAT POSITIONS DETECTED BY
⊙ = DIRECTION FINDING AND DECRYPTING THE GERMAN ENIGMA CODE

29 U-BOAT POSITIONS TRANSMITTED BY CONVOY BETWEEN SEPT 22 AND 26. ALSO

10 REPORTS OF U-BOATS MAKING SIGHTING REPORTS OF R CONVOY OR IMPORTANT UNIT.

ESCORTS R.B.1. (2)

H.M.S. VANOC. SENIOR OFFICER

H.M.S. VETERAN. SUNK

← ST JOHNS
N.F.

1038/23

2309/22

CONVOY SHIPS (8)

S.S. BOSTON. COMMODORE.   SUNK
S.S. NEW YORK. VICE "   SUNK
S.S. YORKTOWN   SUNK
S.S. NEW BEDFORD
S.S. NAUSHON
S.S. NORTHLAND
S.S. SOUTHLAND
S.S. PRESIDENT WARFIELD.

NUMBER OF U-BOATS ATTACKING R.B.1. = 17.

A German grid reference map

October 1st to March 31st. This amount remained unchanged and was withdrawn in 1945.

The main cause for these sub-standard conditions was not dealt with, and it would be only fair to say that it was really impossible to do so. This cause was first and last the gross overcrowding and even one shilling and six pence per day had no effect in reducing it, but perhaps made it more tolerable for six months of the year. These destroyers when built were to have a complement of 134 officers and men, and although this may also be considered overcrowding, hence the "hard lying" money, the crew's number would be the minimum to carry out all the ship's duties and man the armaments etc. at that time.

As the years progressed from 1918, and although the Fleets were reduced, there would always be those who were engaged to produce new and more powerful weapons and fire power, detection of submersed ships, detection of aircraft and surface craft, improved communication systems and so on. The introduction of all these technical improvements to the warships would involve extra trained men to be able to cover the manning of the range of requirements 24 hours a day. This would be a steady and continuous process throughout the war, increasing the complements of all warships. Many ships could absorb this increase, others with tolerable changes, but for ships like V & W destroyers it just became even worse and more primitive. In some V & Ws the ship's complement had increased from the intended 134 men to nearer 170, about 27%, or now four men to every three before. The seamen's mess deck, as previously mentioned, was always well packed and full up with a few more than 40 men, but now had to accommodate another 50% – 60/65 men. Where did they fit in? Well they just didn't. They had to find space for their kit and bedding as best they could. It was ironic that a respite to the overcrowding came when the men were closed up at cruising stations, that is about one third to one half manning all positions, and of course action stations cleared the lot out.

Perhaps some mention should be made of the toilet and washing arrangements. To describe them as facilities would be a sin. The few toilets had to be flushed with salt water, which was pumped up to an overhead gravity tank, kept full in most circumstances but not reliably so. The large number of men obviously caused queuing, and in bad weather when many were sea-sick the hygiene conditions were deplorable. The toilets or "heads" were situated on the main deck below the break of the forecastle on the port side, and strangely not open to the elements. In a similar position on the starboard side was a compartment by the ship's side with the bottom open to the scuppers and a canvas screen inboard. There were "duck boards" on the steel deck with the sea water swishing away quite happily around your feet. I suppose this could be described as the "wash room". There was a metal frame secured to the deck which had six metal bowl attached that could not be removed but had hinges to tip them up. To empty the bowls, you had to tip them out, the water would go into a wooden trough and disappear into the scuppers or if the ship decided, back round your feet. There were no baths or showers, just the six metal bowls for all the men, but this could be supplemented by washing in the mess deck buckets. There was no running water or taps. The water was obtained from the opposite side of the ship of the upper deck. There was a steam kettle for heating the water, the round open top tank held about 20 gallons and had an internal steam coil. The water had to be hand pumped to fill the kettle and the steam supply regulated. The water was drawn off at the lower end into a bucket and shared amongst the other men. The unwritten law was that the last user should always check that the level was high and steam on ready for the other few to use, but as this law was unwritten the opposite was the norm. Cold water came from the same hand pump, all carried from one side of the ship to the other. If this domestic tank had been requisitioned for extra fuel then these mod cons would cease to be. If you had thought that each man had a sparkling fresh bowl of water to wash and shave in, forget it, as each bowl of water was often used as 'twicers', 'thricers' and so on. The good news was that there was an unlimited supply of salt water available 24 hours a day!

Ships are always tenderly called "she", sometimes because

they are so unpredictable, but the old V & Ws behaved like rampant bulls in a raging temper. The movement of these ships in bad weather was fearful. The shape of the bows caused the ship to barge her way through heavy seas instead of riding the waves, causing vast amounts of water to come over the bow and upper decks. The ships were virtually out of sight until they struggled clear again. If the weather became unbearable and the safety of the ship was threatened, speed had to be reduced, hove to or making steerage way only. When pitching heavily every nerve of the ship shuddered, forward gun mountings could be partly un-shipped, ASDIC domes broken off and these ships developed corrugated bottoms with the continuous poundings. There was rarely a time at sea when these ships were comfortable, and they remained frisky in even fair conditions. Once at sea, wire hawsers were fitted each side of the main deck from forward to aft, about six feet high. Short lengths of rope with metal thimbles could run up and down these safety lifelines. Men who had to travel either way for changing shifts and so on, would grasp a line with both hands, watch what the sea was doing and if he considered the waves were not going to wash over, run like hell and pull up his legs when the water was washing over, get a good bashing and finish up a nervous wreck at his destination. Once away there was no turning back half way.

In severe foul conditions, the odds that you would make it home and dry were very high against you and if you were half drowned there was always the consolation that there was someone to have a good laugh at you. By brilliant design the ship's stores, food, rum etc. were situated aft and the mess decks forward, also the officers' quarters were aft and the bridge forward so the lifelines had good use. I have known men to lose stores on these trips, but never the rum issue; a fate worse than death.

However these old V & Ws had their good points. They were extremely hardy, and could handle the most atrocious conditions and come back for more. Although restricted in endurance due to insufficient fuel storage they had a speed that enabled them to attack U-boats and quickly get back to

57

convoy. Their very low draught was a godsend in the evacuation of troops at Dunkirk and the Belgian and Dutch coasts. They had been in their time good fleet screening destroyers and formidable ships to carry out torpedo attacks. They had been used as mine layers, quickly in and out at night, whatever was asked they would be there. In my naval experience they were always recognised by the other naval ships and many merchant ships, and respected. Some merchant ships' crews seemed to have a safer feeling when the escorts had a few V & Ws with them.

In this book the two old V & W destroyers HMS *Vanoc* and HMS *Veteran* participate in the escorting of Convoy R.B.1, and their history is mostly confined to this episode, but they were extremely lucky during the evacuation of Narvik in the Norwegian campaign, in early June 1940. The carrier *Glorious* and her two escorting destroyers HMS *Acasta* and HMS *Ardent* set out for home and were accompanied for a short time by the two ancient V & W destroyers *Veteran* and *Vanoc*. When still off the coast of Norway, the carrier and its two escorts were sunk by a powerful German force which included the battle cruisers *Scharnhorst* and *Gneisenau*, and their destroyer escorts. After this heroic action by such a small force against what was one of the most powerful German battle fleets at sea at that time, the loss of life was very heavy: only one survivor from the two destroyers. Over 300 died as well as the carrier crew with 41 men of the R.A.F., over 1,500. Survivors were very few; only 39, and six rescued and taken P.O.W.

9

Remembrance: HMS Veteran

The loss of HMS *Veteran*, and the total loss of her crew and the survivors she had rescued under such dangerous conditions was once again brought to the notice of the public by a service of remembrance and a memorial dinner, held at Wrexham on Tuesday September 15th 1992, ten days prior to the 50th anniversary of her sinking. This event took place thanks to over two years of dedicated research, both in this country and abroad, of the entire history of HMS *Veteran* by the Wrexham businessman John Lawton. His work will be well worthy of publication some day.

John's dedication to the Wrexham memorial event enabled many people to attend – civic dignitaries, naval representatives from America, Canada and the U.K., old shipmates from previous years, some relatives and family associates of previous captains, a guard of honour and representatives from the Corvettes Association and many others.

The memorial service was held at St Mary's church, Whitewell, Shropshire, the family church of the Warburton Lee family. Captain Warburton Lee R.N. had been associated with the *Veteran* in the 1930s on the China station. He was awarded the Victoria Cross during the Norwegian Campaign. A memorial plaque is situated in the church. It was the family of Captain Warburton Lee who, together with John Lawton and the Reverend P. Winchester, made a most memorable day and excellent service for everyone.

There were only two men present who had been in the North Atlantic with Convoy R.B.1, both serving on the only other escort HMS *Vanoc*. Ray Freeman was a nineteen-year-old signalman and Jim Reed was a twenty-year-old leading seaman/gunner.

10

The U-boat War

North Atlantic 1939–1945

A decision made in May 1945 by the German Grand Admiral
Karl Doenitz, has enabled naval historians worldwide to have
access to German Naval records dating back to 1871. It would
seem that without doubt Doenitz was an efficient and
dedicated naval man and even with ultimate and brutal defeat
staring Germany in the face, he had made plans to preserve
and make safe these vast records for posterity. His worst fear
was that if they fell into Russian hands they would be
destroyed or forever retained in the Soviet archives. So it was
in May 1945, when the German resistance was collapsing and
the Allied troops advancing on all fronts, that Doenitz ordered
that all the German naval records were to be sent immediately
to the Danish border town of Flensburg, well clear of the
Russian forces, and if the final German defeat came, the
records were not to be destroyed but handed over intact to the
British or Americans. These orders were carried out and the
records passed safely into British hands.

Obviously, although the war in Europe had ceased, these
records provided a wealth of information, much of it unknown
to the wartime Allies, and gave a better understanding of the
war at sea. It is believed that all the documents were in later
years returned to the German state archives. These have been
open to the public for many years. The last entry in these
records was April 10th 1945.

In making these brief notes on the Battle of the Atlantic and the U-boat menace, I have found that the decision of Doenitz, and the records saved, have given another view of the most appalling Atlantic war.

On May 8th 1945 Britain's wartime prime minister Winston Churchill despatched the following signal to the fleet:

> For the second time since the Battle of Trafalgar, sea power, relentlessly applied, has preserved and sustained our nation and commonwealth and led to the decisive defeat of Germany and her European associates. The Board of Admiralty congratulates all officers and men upon their share in this great victory, confident that the fortitude, skill and tenacity which have made it possible will be displayed with the same distinction and effect in the task yet to be completed in the Far East.

With due respect to those associated with the sending of this signal, it did not result in joyous rapture among the mess-decks and quarters, just a reminder that the Navy's struggle was not over by a long chalk. But it also meant an end to the Battle of the Atlantic which had gone on for over five and a half years.

This book is not intended to deal at great length with the finer details of the U-boat war in the North Atlantic, but some background is called for here. After the armistice of the Great War, 1914–1918, and the Treaty of Versailles, Germany was forbidden to either build or acquire submarines. By 1932 Germany was fully aware of the submarine arms, of foreign naval powers. The construction plans for building submarines and the ship building facilities were virtually complete and by the end of that year plans had been approved for rebuilding the German Navy. This was to include 16 U-boats, when changes in the political situation allowed. 1933 was the year when what was to be the most alarming sequence of events began. By far the worst of these was at the end of January when the National Socialists came to power. This was followed by the disarmament conference in Geneva in March. By October the German Admiralty, with discussions going on for the rebuilding of the Navy, had decided that the U-boats already planned should now be built.

It was really about five years previously, in 1927, that the prototype of these U-boats had been built and tested in Spain. This was a 750 ton U-boat, which under the Treaty of Versailles, Germany could not own, and so was acquired by Turkey in 1931. In 1935 Germany repudiated the Treaty, announcing her intention to build up her air force, and with an agreement with Britain undertook to keep her naval tonnage to a certain ratio. This applied with various changes to the other ships being constructed. The Germans were so advanced in U-boat construction that they commissioned the first U-boat in Kiel eleven days after signing the agreement. In the next four years, irrespective of agreements or treaties, the U-boat construction programme continued. In September 1939 when World War II commenced, Germany had 46 U-boats ready for operations and a further ten U-boats commissioned and being made ready for operations. It is remarkable that a country that theoretically had no submarines in 1935 had come back with a ship building industry for U-boats alone capable of having 56 operational and a further high production programme in place by 1939. Further, these U-boats were the most modern with the latest technology available at that time.

The Battle of the Atlantic was a sea war that had no equal in history. For almost six years it had been a cruel and savage war of attrition, in thousands of square miles of ocean, in most appalling weather, ferocious gales and low temperatures and extremely difficult living conditions. The hardships and danger everyone experienced were really indescribable. This terrible life was shared by all, be it merchant ships, escorts, patrol aircraft or U-boats. The object of this maritime slaughter of human beings and ships was:

For the allies: To preserve the vital supply life-line from the American and Canadian seaboard across the Atlantic to the United Kingdom, a task that must not fail as the future of the whole free world depended on it. Without food supplies Britain would face starvation and defeat. Without armed forces and supplies coming over to the U.K. there could be no invasion of Europe. A total blockade of Britain would have resulted in capitulation and a way of life too terrible to contemplate.

For the Germans: The total blockade of Britain with the destruction and loss of vital supplies of food and materials, eventually making it impossible to survive or have the ability to retaliate. The losses to the Allies of merchant ships, naval escorts and patrol aircraft ran into millions of tons of shipping and supplies and thousands of lives. For the German Navy the number of U-boats destroyed was very high and the percentage of the crews killed also, but in actual lives lost the numbers were very much lower than those whose ships had been sunk or damaged, or even of their comrades on the Russian front. For the considerable havoc caused continuously over all those years, the debt the people of Germany owed to the U-boat crews are indeed great, and the victory they sought was at times only a whisker away.

To look again at the final figures of U-boat losses at the end of the war in Europe, it is noticeable that historians do not always agree with each other. This is not really a fault, as to compile this information from individual and official records that are available, brings about duplications and errors. Also the dating of the research can have an effect on the calculations. I am sure that these discrepancies are unavoidable, just as the figures being used in this book from German records may also be inaccurate.

U-boat War in the Atlantic, Losses and Causes

Enemy guns, torpedoes, depth charges, mines and bombs	636
Air attack on U-boat bases and yards	63
Collision, internal explosion, mining home waters, other causes	85
Surrendered after capitulation	154
Scuttled by their crews on the eve of surrender	218
TOTAL	1156

It is widely accepted that the U-boat losses exceeded 1,000 including those that surrendered or were scuttled.

Losses of U-boat Crew Members

Total number of U-boat crewmen	40,000	100%
Killed or Missing	28,000	70%
Prisoners of War	5,000	12.5%

Research understandably comes up with a small variation in the figures, so a general compilation has been used.

The U-boat memorial situated near Kiel records the names of 27,491 dead. According to these figures the casualty rate for a group operation and a very long campaign are tremendously high, with approximately seven men out of ten being killed. It is unbelievable that recruitment could continue when the navy men ashore must have been aware of the great loss of their comrades. Some sources gave the life expectancy of a U-boat crewman as not more than three patrols. It is remarkable that just over 5,000 men were saved in such hazardous conditions and shows the character and humanity of the officers and men of those ships engaged in the rescues, even putting the ships and men in a most dangerous position to do so. According to Winston Churchill, "A point of interest was the rescue of the German U-boat ace Lieutenant Commander Otto Kretschmer, when his boat U-99 was sunk by the old 'V & W' destroyer HMS *Walker* in March 1941. Although interned as a P.O.W. for just over four years and continuing his Naval service afterwards, he became head of the Federal German Navy". Churchill believed that the U-boat menace and "the Battle of the Atlantic, was the dominating factor all through the war everything happening depended ultimately on its outcome". No veteran of the Atlantic conflict would disagree with that statement.

The U-boats

The U-boat "numbers" ranged from those commissioned in 1935 to those commissioned in 1945, from U-1 to U-1308. The U-boats mostly encountered in the Atlantic were the Type

VIIC Atlantic U-boat and Type VIIC/41. Both these were 770 tons and were commissioned between 1940 and 1945, totalling 659 U-boats.

The Type VIIC details were approximately as follows: Length 220 feet, beam 20.5 feet, draught 15 to 15.5 feet. Displacement on the surface 770 tons plus 100 tons submerged. Speed 17 to 17.5 knots surfaced and 7.5 knots submerged (duration one hour endurance).

Surfaced:	9,700 miles at 10 knots using diesel-electric with M.A.N. diesels.
	8,850 miles at 10 Knots (cruising) with M.A.N. diesels
	6,500 miles at 12 Knots (cruising) with M.A.N. diesels.
	3,450 miles at 17 Knots (maximum sustained) with M.A.N. diesels.
Submerged:	130 miles at 2 knots
	80 miles at 4 knots
Diving Depth:	309 feet
Armament:	Torpedo tubes – 4 bow, 1 stern
	Outfit – 14 torpedoes (max) 12 (normal)
	Combinations with mines and torpedoes, up to 39 mines
	Guns – 1 × 3.5 inch (88mm)
	1 × 0.8 inch (20mm) A.A. gun
Complement:	44 men

The type VIIC/41 was similar to the VIIC but had an increase in diving depth to almost 400 feet. It can be seen that the Atlantic Type U-boat had been very efficiently designed back in the early 1930s with long endurance and formidable armament, and requiring little modernisation.

The U-boat construction programme during World War II continued at an exceptionally high rate, in spite of the very heavy bombing raids by the Allies on the shipyards and installations. Even three months before the war ceased, the new U-boat building programme was to produce 60 extra U-boats per month and would be entering another serious phase of the sea war with the introduction of the most modern submarines in the world. This new breed had revolutionised the propulsion and armament of ships. Submerged speeds mentioned at that time were greater than the convoys and escorts could produce, and surface speeds even greater. Endurance would be vastly exceeded, as well as diving depths, also the torpedoes could be fired at submerged depths and unobserved. It must have been an enormous relief to the Allied sea forces and convoys that the war on land ceased when it did, before those U-boats could become operational. It is hard to consider how the Battle of the Atlantic would have gone if these U-boats had been operational in the North Atlantic before the "Air Gap" had been closed.

U-boats in Commission and in Operation

At the end of 1939	53	34
At the end of 1940	73	27
At the end of 1941	236	88
At the end of 1942	381	204
At the end of 1943	424	159 (Peaked at 240)
At the end of 1944	409	130 (Peaked at 176)
April 1945	429	166

It shows the tenacity and single mindedness of those involved in the German U-boat business that in six years they built or acquired over 1,300 U-boats and lost almost 800, and yet at the end of the war, in a country in desolation, there was still a potential strength of 400 or more. The industry was also about to produce a submarine type with no equal. But it also shows the bravery and dedication of the Allied sea and air powers and their high efficiency that these U-boats were rendered inoperative.

BIBLIOGRAPHY AND ACKNOWLEDGEMENTS

Crown copyright material in the public record office is reproduced by permission of the Controller of Her Majesty's Stationery Office. P.R.O. document reference ADM 199/1709.

Ministry of Defence (Navy) (1989). The U-boat War in the Atlantic 1939–45. H.M.S.O. 2 volumes.

Imperial War Museum, Lambeth Road, London, SE1 6HZ.

Imperial War Museum, Information/Research Dept., All Saints, Austral Street, London, SW1.

Public Record Office, Ruskin Avenue, Kew, Richmond, Surrey, TW9 4DU.

National Maritime Museum, Greenwich, London, SE10 9NF.

The Maritime History Group, Memorial University of Newfoundland, St. John's, N.F., Canada, AIC 557.

Maritime Museum of the Atlantic, 1675 Lower Water Street, Halifax, N.S., Canada., Dept. of Education and Culture.

Washington D.C. Declassified Signals. Authority NND 968133.

German Naval Archives. Berlin, Germany

Chronology of the War at Sea, 1939–1945. Jürgen Rohwer and G. Hummelchen.

British Merchant Vessels Lost or Damaged by Enemy Action During WWII 3.9.1939–2.9.1945. (1947). H.M.S.O. London.

Ships of the Royal Navy, Statement of Losses During WWII 3.9.1939–2.9.1945. (1947) H.M.S.O. London.

Merchant Navy, Memorial List, Tower Hill, London.

Admiralty Trade Division Records, H.M.S.O.

Steam Packets on the Chesapeake. Published U.S.A., date unknown.

Sea Breezes, December 1946.

The Shipping World, June 13th 1945.

The Log Line, London. Winter 1948.

Washington D.C. *Sunday Star*, May 20th 1945.

Official History; War at Sea. Vols. 1–3. H.M.S.O.

History of U.S. Naval Operations in WWII, Vol. 1, The Battle of the Atlantic. (1970). Samuel Eliot Morrison.

Far Distant Ships, Canadian Naval Operations WWII. Joseph Schull. Date unknown

Axis Submarine Successes 1939–1945. Jürgen Rohwer.

Transatlantic Convoy Routes Agreed Upon by U.S. Navy and British Admiralty. Those in Operation 1942, Maps, Sketches.

ABBREVIATIONS

COMINCH (C + R)	C in C U.S. Fleet
	Washington convoy and routing section
COMNAVEU	Commander of U.S. Naval Forces in Europe
T.F. or T.G.	Task Force or Task Group. Allied Navy
C.T.F.24	Commander Task Force 24 = Convoy R.B.1
C.T.G.24.7	Commander Task Group 24.7
CinCWA	C in C Western Atlantic 24.7 Liverpool
C.O.A.C.	Commanding Officer Atlantic Coast. Halifax, N.S.
F.O.N.F.	Fleet Officer Newfoundland. St. John's N.F.
N.O.I.C.	Naval Officer in Command
N.S.H.Q.	Nova Scotia Head Quarters. Halifax, Ottawa
N.C.S.O.	Naval Command Senior Officer. St. John's N.F.
N.M.C.J.S.	Naval Member Canadian Joint Staff. Washington
H.M.C.S. WASH	Canadian Naval Service. Washington
C.C.N.F.	Commander (central command) N.F.
O.P.N.A.V.	Operations North Atlantic. Code Room
COMAMPHORLANT	Command. Atlantic
BUSHIPS	Bolero U.S. Ships
BAD	Battle Atlantic Decrypting
BOLERO	Operation code name for the build up of American forces in Britain, prior to the invasion of Europe from 1942
TORCH	Code name for the Allied landings in France North Africa, November 11th 1942

H.F./D.F.	High Frequency / Direction Finding
M.O.M.P.	Mid Ocean meeting point
RASPBERRY	Deploying convoy formation and firing starshells to locate U-boats on the surface
ENIGMA	The German coding machine
ULTRA	The Allies top secret system for deciphering Enigma
B-DIENST	The German decoding system for Allies signals

An explanation of "Raspberry" mentioned in signals of convoy R.B.1. Extract from '*Battle of the Atlantic*' – Convoy Tactics.

If a U-boat got close enough to launch its torpedoes undetected in a night attack, the explosion would trigger off a pre-arranged sequence of counter measures known as "Raspberries", "Artichokes", and "Buttercups". On the appropriate signal from the senior escort officer, the escorts nearer the attacker would fire "Snowflake" illuminant rockets and carry out sweeps to drive the U-boat under so that it became vulnerable to ASDIC before it could use its high surface speed to escape. The sweeps and subsequent ASDIC hunts would be carried out until the U-boat was destroyed or forced well astern of the convoy, but counter measures had to be judged according to the scale of the attack, since vulnerable gaps could be left in the defences which other U-boats would be able to exploit and the escort commander had to remember that his first duty was the safe and timely arrival of the convoy.

APPENDIX 1

The Ships of Convoy R.B.1

The eight ships were known as British, being the SS *Boston*, SS *New York*, SS *Yorktown*, SS *Northland*, SS *Southland*, SS *President Warfield*, SS *Naushon* and SS *New Bedford*.

Boston No 223749 and **New York No 223901 (Twin screw steamers)**
Company: Eastern Steamship Lines Incorp. Boston, Massachusetts, U.S.A.
Built: 1924 by Bethlehem Shipbuilding Corp, Sparrows Point, Maryland, U.S.A.
Dimensions: 385.3 ft length, 72.5 ft breadth, 20.9 ft depth, 4989 gross, 2703 net tons.
Engines: Four steam turbines, single reduction geared to two shafts. Built by Bath Ironworks, Bath, Maine.
Speed: 19 knots.
History: With the opening of the Cape Cod Canal, the Eastern Steamship Lines started a direct service between Boston and New York in 1924 with these two passenger ships as overnight boats alternating between these ports.
December 29th 1941, sold to the U.S. Government.
July 21st 1942, under the lend-lease agreement both ships were turned over to the British M.W.T., flying "The Red Duster" in place of "Old Glory" with the added title of SS (Steamship) to their names; SS *Boston* and SS *New York*.
These ships of shoal draught, designed and built as inland waters pleasure boats and considered totally unsuitable to cross the North Atlantic were docked in the U.S. and by extra strengthening and massive timber boarding up of the open decks and sides were to become part of Convoy R.B.1, codename "Maniac".
September 21st 1942, SS *Boston* **Captain R.S. Young**, Commodore and SS *New York* **Captain C. Mayers**, Vice Commodore left St. John's N.F. during the most critical stage of the U-boat war. During

several days of very heavy U-boat attacks the SS *New York* was sunk September 25th, and the SS *Boston* on September 26th.

The Eastern Steamship Lines did not restore the full service again after the end of the war.

Naushon No 1978/29 (Twin screw steamship)

Company: New England Steamship Company, New Bedford, Mass., U.S.A.

Built: 1929 by Bethlehem Shipbuilding Corp, Quincy, Mass., U.S.A.

Dimensions: 250 ft length, 45 ft breadth, 16 ft depth. 1978 gross, 936 net tons.

Engines: 2 x 4 cylinder, triple-expansion, 100 N.H.P. by shipbuilder.

History: Short run service, New Bedford, Martha's Vineyard, Nantucket Island.

1942, transfer to U.S. War Shipping Administration. September 9th 1942 transfer to British M.W.T. from the U.S. W.S.A.

Conversion: by U.S. to protect structure from the heavy weather to be encountered in a North Atlantic crossing: strengthening, timber boarding, fitting guns.

September 21st 1942 under the command of **Captain J.J. Murray**, left St. John's N.F. as part of Convoy R.B.1, "Maniac" to Londonderry, U.K. Made it independently to the north coast of Scotland.

Restructured in U.K. as Royal Navy "Hospital Ship 49". Used as hospital ship and troop carrier in and around the English Channel and later became a veteran of the Normandy invasion. The SS *Naushon* carried the first casualties from the action back to England.

June 20th 1945 returned to the U.S. Maritime Commission.

1947 sold to Meseck Steamboat Co. of New York, renamed *John A. Meseck* and operated as a New York Harbour excursion steamer.

Yorktown No 1547/28 (Single screw steamship)

Company: Chesapeake Steamship Company, Baltimore, U.S.A.

Built: 1928 by Newport News Shipbuilding and Drydock Co. Newport News, Virginia.

Dimensions: 267 ft length, 46 ft breadth, 18 ft depth, 1547 gross, 817 net tons.

Engines: Triple-expansion, 4 cylinder, 270 N.H.P. by shipbuilder.

History: 1941, sold to Baltimore Steam Packet Co, Baltimore, Maryland.

Employed on ferry excursion routes, Chesapeake Bay. Operated in overnight service.

July 11th 1942 transfer to British Ministry of War transport as SS *Yorktown*.

Conversion: In a U.S. Atlantic coast port to protect structure from the heavy weather to be encountered in a North Atlantic crossing, strengthening, timber boarding, fitting guns.

September 21st 1942 under the command of **Captain W.P. Boylan** left St. John's N.F., as part of Convoy R.B.1, codename "Maniac", for Londonderry, U.K.

September 26th 1942, 2050 hours, speed 12.3 knots, travelling independently, torpedoed and sunk.

New Bedford No 1116/28 (Single screw steamship)

Company: New England Steamship Company, New Bedford, Massachusetts, U.S.A.

Built: 1928 by Bethlehem Shipbuilding Corp, Quincy, Massachusetts.

Dimensions: 202 ft 6 ins length, 36 ft 2 ins breadth, 13 ft depth. 1116 gross, 451 net tons.

Engines: Triple-expansion, 4 cylinder, 88 N.H.P. by shipbuilders.

Service: The *New Bedford* and the *Naushon* were built to carry passengers, freight and automobiles from the mainland to the islands of Martha's Vineyard and Nantucket off the coast of Massachusetts. Transfer in 1942 to the U.S. Maritime Commission.

Conversion: In a U.S. Atlantic coast port to protect structure from the heavy weather to be encountered in a North Atlantic crossing. After deck cut down for anti-submarine gun mounting, forward deck and sides enclosed with timber boarding.

August 4th 1942 transfer to British Ministry of War Transport. Lend-lease, for use as hospital ship/troop carrier as SS *New Bedford*.

September 21st 1942 under the command of **Captain R. Hardy** left for St. John's N.F. as part of Convoy R.B.1, "Maniac", for Londonderry, U.K. Reconstructed in the U.K. as a military hospital carrier for war service during the invasion of Europe.

June 20th 1945 returned to the ownership of U.S. Maritime Commission.

1949, purchased by Sound Steamship Lines Incorp., Long Island, New York. In service Long Island Sound, passenger and excursion.

June 1967 sold to John J. Witte, Marine Salvage Yard, Staten Island, New York, and 1996 was still laying up as scrap.

Southland No 2081/08 (Single screw steamship)

Company: Norfolk and Washington Steamboat Co., Washington, D.C., U.S.A.

Built: 1908 by Harlan and Hollingsworth Corp., Wilmington, Delaware.

Dimensions: 291 ft 2 in length, 51 ft breadth, 16 ft 1 in depth. 2081 gross, 1215 net tons (later to 3117 tons).

Engines: Triple-expansion, 4 cylinder, 240 N.H.P., by shipbuilders.

Service: Norfolk / Newport News / Chesapeake Bay ports. Chesapeake night boat.

Conversion: In a U.S. Atlantic coast port to protect structure from the heavy weather to be encountered in a North Atlantic crossing, by heavy timber boarding up to the open decked plan forward deck and sides. Also fitted armaments of 1 x 12 PDR anti-submarine gun, 4 Oerlikons, 4 P.A.C. rockets, 10 smoke floats and 1 Ross Rifle. Transfer in 1942 to the U.S. Maritime Commission.

July 9th 1942 transfer to British M.W.T. as SS *Southland*.

September 21st 1942 under the command of **Captain John Williams**, left St. John's N.F. as part of Convoy R.B.1, "Maniac", for Londonderry, U.K. After crossing, operated as personnel ship, then converted on the Thames early 1943 to accommodation ship for the Royal Navy based at Inverary, combined operations centre.

May 22nd 1944 returned to U.S. War Shipping Administration and served with U.S. Forces in Europe.

1947, sold to Fu Chung Corp. (China) Ltd. renamed *Hung Yung*.

1950, sold to Lee International Corp., China.

1955, sold to Hong Kong ship breakers, work starting May 1955.

Northland No 2055/11 (Single screw steamship)

Company: Norfolk and Washington Steamboat Co., Washington, D.C., U.S.A.

Built: 1911 by Harlan and Hollingsworth Corp., Wilmington, Delaware.

Dimensions: 291 ft 2 in length, 51 ft breadth, 18 ft 6 in depth. 2055 gross, 1205 net tons (later to 3336 tons).

Engines: Triple-expansion, 4 cylinder, 240 N.H.P. by shipbuilders.

Service: Norfolk / Newport News / Chesapeake Bay night boat. Transfer in 1942 to the U.S. Maritime Commission.

Conversion: In a U.S. Atlantic coast port to protect structure from the heavy weather to be encountered in a North Atlantic crossing, by heavy boarding up of the open decked plan. Also fitted a 12 PDR anti-submarine gun, 4 Oerlikons, 4 P.A.C. rockets, 1 Rifle and Smoke Floats i.e. 1 Ross Rifle (these conversions gave a completely different profile).

July 11th 1942 transferred to the British M.W.T. as SS *Northland*.
September 21st 1942 under the command of **Captain J. Beckett O.B.E.**, left St. John's N.F. as part of Convoy R.B.1, "Maniac", for Londonderry, U.K.
Converted on the Thames as accommodation ship for the Royal Navy and based at Inverary, combined operations centre. Returned to the U.S. War Shipping Administration May 22nd 1944 and taken over by the U.S. Navy as USS *Leydon* for service during the invasion of Europe.

President Warfield No 1814/28 (Single screw steamship)

Company: Baltimore Steam Packet Co., Baltimore, Maryland. (Named after S. Davies Warfield, head of the seaboard).
Built: 1928 by Pusey and Jones Corp., Wilmington, Delaware.
Dimensions: 320 ft length, 56 ft 6 in breadth, 16 ft 9 in depth. 1814 gross, 706 net tons.
Engines: Triple-expansion, 4 cylinder, 286 N.H.P. by shipbuilders.
Service: Operated overnight service on Chesapeake Bay between Baltimore and Norfolk. Employed on ferry excursion routes. Considered the Old Bay Line flagship. 1942, transfer to U.S. War Shipping Administration.
Conversion: In a U.S. Atlantic coast port to protect structure from the heavy weather to be encountered in a North Atlantic crossing, by heavy boarding up of the open decked plan and sides. Also fitted a 12 PDR anti-submarine gun, Oerlikons, plus other armament items fitted.
July 12th 1942 transfer to British M.W.T as SS *President Warfield*.
September 21st 1942 under the command of **Captain J.R. Williams**, left for St. John's N.F. as part of Convoy R.B.1, "Maniac", to Londonderry, U.K.
March 1943 converted in Southampton to accommodation ship for the Royal Navy based at Instow, near Bideford, losing half her speed of 16 knots.
July 1943 returned to U.S. Navy as USS *President Warfield* and became an assault boat training base for U.S. Forces with quarters for 105 officers and 500 men. Later to storm the beaches of France.
April 1944 moved to Barry Roads, D-Plus-30 day crossed to Omaha Beach to serve as a station and accommodation ship for harbour control.
May 20th 1944 returned to U.S. War Shipping Administration.
1947 sold to Potomac Ship Wrecking Co. for demolition, but resold

to unknown Israeli interests, renamed *Exodus* or *Exodus from Europe*.
July 18th 1947 carried 4,493 illegal immigrants to Palestine from France.
August 26th 1952 damaged by fire at Haifa, beached and later broken up.

Three ships that were destined to form part of Convoy R.B.1 but did not make it were:

John Cadwalader 1478 tons. 1926
Built for Baltimore and Philadelphia Steamboat Co. and sold to Ericsson Line Inc., Baltimore.
July 28th 1942 transfer to British Ministry of War Transport.
August 29th 1942 total loss by fire at Philadelphia.

Colonel J.A. Moss 842 tons. 1925
Built for Steamer Belle Island Co. Incorporated, New York as *Belle Island* and operated as a lower Hudson excursion steamer.
1942 taken over by U.S. Army and renamed *Colonel J.A. Moss.*
July 1942 reached Halifax N.S. but found unsuitable to attempt a North Atlantic crossing.
February 16th 1943 returned to the U.S. and sold to Ary Cesar, Burlamaque, Brazil and renamed *Maria de Lourdes.*

Virginia Lee 2158 tons. 1928
Built for Pennsylvania Railroad Co., later the New York Philadelphia and Norfolk Railroad Co.
July 9th 1942 transfer to British M.W.T. but found unsuitable to attempt an Atlantic crossing.
February 10th 1943 returned to the U.S. and sold to B.B. Wills Line Inc., renamed *Holiday* and fitted with oil engines.
1951 sold to Virginia Ferry Co. and converted to a car ferry, tonnage increased to 4615 tons, renamed *Accomac.*

During the period of lend-lease arrangements, U.S. to the M.W.T., the management of all the eight vessels of Convoy R.B.1 was placed in the hands of Coast Lines Ltd, Liverpool, experts in the management of coastal passenger vessels.

78

APPENDIX 2

U-boats Taking Part in the Attack on Convoy R.B.1

These consisted of two groups forming patrol lines.

Vorwarts Group 10 U-boats, Type VIIC Atlantic U-boat, all commissioned between 1941 and 1944: U-91, U-582, U-619, U-211, U-380, U-584, U-404, U-96, U-260, and U-407
Pfiel Group 7 U-boats, 6 of Type VIIC Atlantic U-boat and 1 of VIID 690 ton Atlantic U-boat minelayer, all commissioned between 1941 and 1944: U-216, U-356, U-595, U-410, U-607, U-617, and U-618

The Two U-boat Groups

Group	U-boat	Commander	Sinkings
Vorwarts	U-91	Walkerling	–
	U-96	Hellriegel	SS *New York*
	U-211	Hauser	–
	U-260	Purkhold	–
	U-380	Rother	–
	U-404	Von Bulow	HMS *Veteran*
	U-407	Bruller	–
	U-582	Schulte	–
	U-584	Deecke	–
	U-619	Makowski	SS *Yorktown*
Pfiel	U-216	Schultz	SS *Boston*
	U-356	Wallas	–
	U-410	Sturm	–
	U-595	Quaet-Faslem	–
	U-607	Mengerson	–
	U-617	Brandi	–
	U-618	Baberg	–

Although during the counter attacks by Convoy R.B.1 some damage may have been caused, no U-boats were sunk. But before the end of the Atlantic war every one had been destroyed. The following gives details of their last patrols.

U-91 Sailed from France 25.1.1944. Lost 25.2.1944 by escorts *Affleck, Gore* and *Gould*, North Atlantic.

U-582 Sailed from France 14.9.1942. Lost 5.10.1942 by aircraft of 269 squadron, south of Iceland.

U-619 Sailed from Germany 10.9.1942. Lost 15.10.1942 by Hudson N of 269 squadron, North Atlantic, depth charges and gunfire.

U-211 Sailed from France 14.10.1943. Lost 19.11.1943 by aircraft of 179 squadron, North Atlantic.

U-380 Sailed from France 5.11.1942. Lost 11.3.1944 by U.S. Army bombing air raid, Toulon.

U-584 Sailed from France 2.9.1943. Lost 21.10.1943 by aircraft from U.S. carrier USS *Card*, North Atlantic.

U-404 Sailed from France 24.7.1943. Lost 27.7.1943 by aircraft from U.S. Army Anti-sub squadron No 4 and R.A.F. Squadron 224 – Bay patrols, Bay of Biscay.

U-96 Destroyed 30/31.3.1945 by bombing of B-24s U.S. 8th Air Force, Wilhelmshaven.

U-260 Sailed from Norway 21.2.1945. Lost 12.3.1945 by contact or antenna mine and scuttled, Irish coast.

U-407 Sailed from France 2.11.1942. Lost 19.9.1944 returned to Mediterranean by Naval vessels *Troubridge, Terpsichore* and *Garland*, North of Crete.

U-216 Sailed from Germany 29.8.1942. Lost 20.10.1942 by aircraft 224 squadron, Bay of Biscay.

U-356 Sailed from France 5.12.1942. Lost 27.12.1942 by joint four R.C.N. escorts, North Atlantic.

U-595 Sailed from France 31.10.1942. Lost 14.11.1942 by aircraft of 500 squadron, off Algiers.

U-410 Sailed from France 26.4.1943. Lost 11.3.1944 returned to Mediterranean, by bombing U.S. Army air raid, Toulon.

U-607 Sailed from France 10.7.1943. Lost 13.7.1943 by aircraft of 228 squadron, Bay air patrol, Bay of Biscay.

U-617 Sailed from France 28.8.1943. Lost 11.9.1943 returned to Mediterranean, by aircraft of 179 squadron and Naval vessels *Hyacinth, Harlem* and *Woolongong* – air/sea patrols, western Mediterranean.

U-618 Sailed from France 11.8.1944. Lost 14.8.1944 damaged by liberator of 534 squadron and sunk by Naval vessels *Duckworth* and *Essington*, English Channel.

The U-boat U-407 was one of the 17 U-boats that engaged the Convoy R.B.1 in September 1942. One of the ships sunk was falsely identified as the troop transport SS *Viceroy of India*. This U-boat had been transferred to the Mediterranean during Operation "Torch" and it was on 11.11.1942 that the meeting really took place and the transport was sunk. Homeward bound after discharging troops at Algiers, she was sunk off Oran. Another troop transport falsely identified in a further sinking was the SS *Reina del Pacifico*. She also took part in Operation "Torch", landing troops on the beaches east of Oran.

APPENDIX 3

U.S.A. National Archives. Declassified NND-968133 Signals

14.8.1942   COMINCH to Buships, Comamphorlant, (passed by Opnav)

141543   Request availability shallow draught ferries or excursion type ships capable of crossing ocean minimum speed 15 knots to accompany torch convoy be urgently investigated and information furnished COMNAVEU earliest possible date.

17.8.1942   Your 141543 availability ships mentioned carefully explored for 'Bolero' total of eleven ships being prepared
172043   to sail U.K. August and early September speeds 13 and one half knots. Doubtful these vessels can accompany fast convoy. British ministry of transports has full particulars. No other vessels this type available.

18.9.1942   FONF to Admiralty, SBONWAT, bad, FOC Iceland, HMCS Wash, NSHQ, COMMINCH, CinCWA, GESF, CTF24.

1819/16
NCR9253   Sailed 1100z/16. Nine river steamers escorted by HMS *Vanoc* and HMS *Veteran* to St. John's Newfoundland routed through (1) 44.30N L 61.00W (M) 46.20 52.30 (N) 47.31 52.15 speed 12 knots. ETA St. John's Newfoundland 1000z/18. When ready for passage request nine river steamers be sailed to Iceland escorted by HMS Vanoc and HMS Veteran for onward routing to United Kingdom.

19.9.1942   Senior officer of escort considers river steamers can make passage to Londonderry direct, as result of experience on passage to St. John's Newfoundland, I concur. Ships less
14552/19   Virginia Lee will be ready to sail A.M. Monday 21st

September. Propose to sail them direct by great circle to Londonderry. Request early concurrence. Propose sailing Virginia Lee when defects completed. Escorted by Thirlmere to Iceland by great circle for onward routing. Ship will probably be ready by Wednesday September 23rd.

19.9.1942   1827z/19 similar information as 1455z/19

22.9.1942   Admiralty to previous distribution plus Commodore Londonderry

1803z/21   My 1455/19 sailed HMS Vanoc and HMS Veteran escorting river steamers less Virginia Lee routed to Londonderry direct by great circle.

22.9.1942   From – NCSO St. John's Newfoundland
To – distribution concerned (Admiralty 1807z/21)
Info – CONNAV, NSHQ, CTF24, NOIC Londonderry from NCSO St. John's Newfoundland

1810z.21	(1)	R.B.1	
	(2)	1800z/21	
	(4)	12 knots	
	(5)	(J)	47.19N52.01W
		(K)	50.33 44.59
		(L)	53.14 34.38
		(M)	54.50 25.02
		(N)	55.29 17.59
		(O)	55.37 10.12
		(P)	55.39 07.40
	(6)		159-12 HMS Veteran
	(7)		5 Columns 2 2 1 2 1
	(8)	(S)	49.15N47.21W
		(T)	51.54 41.55
		(U)	52.25 36.08
		(V)	54.?? 29.51
		(W)	54.42 21.12
		(X)	55.56 12.35 (13)

Commodore master SS Boston
Vice Commodore master SS New York
(14) (19) (20) S.P. 02406 (174) (15)

Newfoundland Code word   124   MANIAC

22.9.1942   Ref. FONF 1455.19
List ships involved less Virginia Lee

221603

22.9.1942   From – COMINCH C + R,
Action for CTU 24-01-18 (case 1), HMS Veteran, CTF24,
FONF.
COAC. NSHQ. Admiralty

221858   Action CTF 14-01-18 HMS Veteran
Info – CTF24 FONF N.F., COAC Halifax ... Admiralty
Estimated 1900V22 PCS R.B.1 ten ships
50.12, 46.15, 060 Twelve altering ... 50.30
44.59 To 53.14. 34.38 x O.N.130 about 30 ships
51.52 39.39 251 51xx

22.9.1942   From – FONF
To – HMS Vanoc CTF24 + Distribution.

1737z/22   NU and AH Altering course forthwith to 090 Degrees for
8 Hours then resumes great circle course for London.

23.9.1942   From – NCSO Great Yarmouth
To – HMS Highlander, S.O 3rd Escort Grp, COMINCH,
C + R.
CTF24, ADM, CinCWA, N.S.H.D FONF, COAC

2331z/22   Your 2250z addressed HMS *Veteran* 875. R.B.1.
49.48 N 46.00 W. 090 11 Alter 065 at 0230z/23

23.9.1942   From – COMINCH (F36)
To – HMS Highlander, USS Monomoy, HMS Vanoc.

230113   U-boat position by DF at 2309z/22 over 150 miles
49.50 N 45 W. Enigma

23.9.1942   To HMS Vanoc, HMS Highlander.
Urgent U-boat warning.

232239   U-boat estimated your vicinity by DF at 1347z/23 has
made sighting of a convoy or important unit. Enigma

23.9.1942   To – HMS Vanoc, CTF24.
231405   U-boat position by DF at 1038z/23 within 150 miles
46.15 N 37.45 W. Enigma

23.9.1942   From – COMINCH, (F-35).
To – HMS Vanoc, HMS Highlander, USS Monomoy,

U-boat position by DF at 1220z/23 within 150 miles
51.15 N 46.00 W Enigma

23.9.1942 From – COMINCH
To – HMS Vanoc
Urgent U-boat Warning.
232027 U-boat estimated your area by DF at 2002z/23
has made sighting report of convoy or important unit.

23.9.1942 From –
To – HMS Vanoc, HMS Highlander, HMS Monomoy.
231949 U-boat position by DR at 1819z/23
within 150 miles 51 N 37 W

23.9.1942 From – COAC
To – Distribution (not clear photocopy)
2135z/23 Refers to Colonel James Moss T.O.A. and proposes that
Virginia Lee and Thirlmere await arrival.

1441z/23 (2) C.O. Atlantic Coast Halifax
To – Report expected time Colonel James A Moss can
arrive
St. John's Newfoundland

23.9.1942 U-boat D.F. Position (unclear)
1453z/23

23.9.1942 Sailing telegram for SS Colonel James A Moss
2107z/23

23.9.1942 From – BAD
To – FONF, COAC, ADM, COMINCH, N.M.C.S
2159z/23 Your 1441/23 Ministry of war transport states that
Colonel James A Moss is un-seaworthy and should not
make passage until early summer.

Res 1441/23 Propose Virginia Lee and Thirlemere be held
at St. John's Newfoundland to await arrival Colonel
James A Moss. C.C. Atlantic coast, Halifax to report
ETA at St. John's Newfoundland

24.9.1942 From – CTU 24-01-18
To – CTF24, ADM, CinCWA, N.S.H.G., COAC,
CONF, CTG24.7, HMS Vanoc, HMS Veteran, Escort
HX208

85

0045z/24	Admiralty's 2228A/23, HF/DF bearings suggest R.B.1 or possible HX208 reported
24.9.1942 241126	To HMS Vanoc U-boat position by DF at 0830z/24 within 150 miles 54N 32.30 W
241321	To HMS Vanoc, HMS Hesperus U-boat position by DF at 0848z/24 uncertain 52.30 N 37.30 W Enigma.
24.9.1942	From – COMINCH, (F35), To – HMCS Saguenway, HMS Vanoc, CTF24.
241359	U-boat position by DF at 1128z/24 uncertain 55.15 N 31.45 W Enigma another by DF at 0938z/24 uncertain 51.30 N 34.00 W Enigma
24.9.1942 241546	U-boat position by DF at 1140z within 150 miles 53.00 N 34.15 W Enigma
24.9.1942	To – HMS Vanoc, HMS Hesperus, CTF24. Urgent U-boat warning. U-boat estimated your vicinity by DF at 0916z/24 had made sighting report on convoy or important unit
24.9.1942	To – HMS Vanoc, HMCS Saguenay, CTF24, CinCLANT U-boat Warning
241725	U-boat position by DF at 1252z/24 within 150 miles 53 N 35 W Alpha. Sighting report. Another at 1240z/24 within 150 miles 53.30 N 31.30 W. Enigma.
24.9.1942 242012	U-boat position by DF at 1706z/24 54.00 N 27.15 W Uncertain Enigma
23.9.1942	From – HMS Vanoc To – CinCWA, Info – CINNAV, CTF24, ADM, N.S.H.Q, FONF, COAC, CTG24-7, FOCI R.B.1 was shadowed from ahead all last night and suspect shadowing continues today Thursday. Escort have insufficient fuel to carry out putting down sweep. Evasive tactics proved useless in extreme visibility with

86

full moon. Air cover would be appreciated as soon as possible PCS 53.14 N 35.20 W (A) 074-12. Request final destination convoy.

25.9.1942	From – HMS Vanoc
	To – HMS Shearwater
01587/25	Carried out 2 attacks A/S contact classified sub in position 53.52N 31.46 W. contact lost after 2nd attack. Rejoining convoy.

25.9.1942	From – HMS Vanoc
	Urgent U-boat Warning
	U-boat estimated your vicinity by DF at 0501z/25 and 0625z/25 has made sighting report of convoy or important unit.

25.9.1942	From – COMINCH
	To – HMS Saguenay, HMS Vanoc
	Urgent U-boat Warning
250339	U-boat estimated your vicinity by DF at 0304z.25 has made sighting report of a convoy or important unit. Alpha.

25.9.1942	From –
	To – HMS Vanoc
	Urgent U-boat Warning
251111	U-boat estimated your vicinity by DF at 1038z/25 has made sighting report of convoy or important unit. Enigma

25.9.1942	From – CTU24-1-16
	To – HMS Vanoc, HMS Veteran
	Information
1115z/25	COMINCH's 0903/25 from locality evidently this sighting report was of convoy R.B.1.

25.9.1942	U-boat position by DF at 1015z.25 within 150 miles
251357	56.45 N 25.15 W Enigma

25.9.1942	U-boat position by DF at 0923z.25 within 150 miles
251405	53.45 N 29.30 W Enigma

25.9.1942	U-boat position by DF at 0956/25 within 150 miles
251413	55.15 N 27.45 W.

25.9.1942	U-boat position by DF at 1056z.25 within 150 miles
251436	54.15 N 28.30 W
	U-boat position by DF at 1038z/25 within 150 miles
	54.45 N 27.45 W Enigma

25.9.1942	U-boat position by DF at 1132z/25 within 150 miles
251456	54.45 N 26.30 W another 1134z/25
	54.15 N 30.30 W another 1213z/25
	54.15 N 27.45 W

| 25.9.1942 | R.D.F. fix at 1256z/25 over 150 miles |
| 251540 | 54.15 N 27.30 W Indicates possibility surface raider in area |

| 25.9.1942 | U-boat position by DF at 1359z/25 within 75 miles |
| 251631 | 54.30 N 28.45 W Enigma |

25.9.1942	From – HMS Vanoc
	To – Previous distribution groups
	R.B.1 attacked. Boston sunk position 54.23 N 27.54 W
	Further report follows

25.9.1942	From – COMINCH
	To – HMS Vanoc, CTF24, CinC lant.
	U-boat position by DF at 1240z/25 within 150 miles
	54.45 N 27 W.
	U-boat by DF at 1424z/25 within 150 miles 54 N 31 W
	Enigma
251742	U-boat position by DF at 1438z/25 within 150 miles
	54.15 N 28.45 W
251856	U-boat estimated your vicinity by DF at 1653z/25
	has made sighting report of convoy or important unit.
251928	U-boat position by DF at 1702z/25 within 150 miles
	55.15 N 27 W
	Enigma
252009	U-boat position by DF at 1801z/25 within 150 miles
	54.30 N 28 W
	Enigma
251811	U-boat position by DF at 1520z/25 within 150 miles
	54.45 N 27 W
	Alpha. U-boat position by DF at 1550z/25 within 150 miles
	54.30 N 28.30 W

25.9.1942   From – CinCWA
To – HMS Sabre, HMS Scimitar, HMS Saladin
Info – HMS Vanoc, HMS Veteran, Stork, ADM 552, COMINCH, FONS, CTF24.
Escort O.N.132. 20th ES.FR. If you have completed with fuelling proceed reinforcement R.B.1 in 54.23 N 27.54 W at 1340zed 25th routed through 54.51 N 25.01 W and 55.31 N 17.59 W speed 12 knots. Report action taken.

25.9.1942   From – COMINCH
To – HMS Vanoc, CTF24, ADM
252137   U-boat position by DF at 1812z/25 within 150 miles 54.30 N 26 W.
Enigma.

25.9.1942   From – HMS Vanoc
To – COMINCH (C + R), CTF24, ADM, N.S.H.Q., FONF, COAC, CTG24.7
1855z/25   My 1340 N 25th search for U-boat has failed. HMS Veteran has 48 survivors including master New Bedford has 2 survivors 1 dead 15 missing presumed killed. Total crew 66. Escort will have rejoined convoy by 2000z

25.9.1942   From – HMS Vanoc
To – CinCWA
Info – CTF24, COMINCH, C + R, ADM, N.S.H.Q., FONF, COAC, CTG24.7, HMS Veteran
0056z/25   My 2110 N R.B.1 New York torpedoed and possible one other New York floated but has since been sunk by further attacks.
HMS Veteran was unnoticed by sub. Now rejoining. 30 survivors including master. Raspberry drew blank. Convoy became disorganised in attack. Have broadcast instructions to them to steer 81 and reform at daylight. Fuel situation of escort becoming shaky.
Position 2110 N 54.34 North 25.44 West. Weather reported.

Convoy   R.B.1
Sailed   St. John's 1800z/21.9.42
Destination   Londonderry
Speed   12 Knots
Escort   HMS Vanoc, HMS Veteran (sunk)
Total ships in Convoy 8

SS Boston	Commodore	Sunk
SS New York	Vice Commodore	Sunk
SS Yorktown		Sunk
SS New Bedford		
SS Naushon		
SS Northland		
SS Southland		
SS President Warfield		

Note   The above ships plus Virginia Lee sailed from Halifax 1100z/16 September
Arrived St. John's Newfoundland 18th September, Escorted HMS *Vanoc* and HMS *Veteran*.

Total of 60 photocopies from Washington National Archives received. Information not yet received or available would be:
1. Sinking of HMS *Veteran*.
2. Sinking of SS *Yorktown*.
3. Arrivals in U.K., dates and ports.

APPENDIX 4

*Reports/Interviews by Master/Chief Officer of
S.S. Yorktown, Northland and Southland*

U-BOAT ATTACK ON CONVOY. - 25.9.42. (Number of convoy not known) RB 1.

s.s. "YORK TOWN" (British) 1751 Gr. tons.

The following account of an attack on an eastbound convoy which left Newfoundland on 21.9.42 has been given by Mr. H.L. PAPKORTH, Chief Officer of the above ship which was sunk. This same attack was reported in our PL 22/5888, PL 22/5889 and PL 7/5747.

At 14.30 hours on 25.9.42, the s.s. "BOSTON" was without warning struck by two torpedoes, one forward in the bow and the other aft. She sank in approximately seven minutes.

No. of ship in convoy	- No. 31.
Date	- 25.9.42.
Time	- 14.30 hrs.
Speed	- 12 knots.
Course	- 0.81
Escort	- 2 destroyers (1 sunk).

All lifeboats were seen to be lowered and the remainder of the convoy scattered at full speed.

A number of torpedo tracks were seen, one ahead and another astern of the s.s. "YORK TOWN". The s.s. "PRESIDENT WARFIELD" opened fire at these tracks but without visible effect.

At about 18.00 hrs. on the same day, the convoy re-formed and proceeded at a speed of 9 knots, and zig-zag No. 40.

Shortly after the reforming of the convoy, the steering gear of the s.s. "YORK TOWN" fouled, and the Captain decided to drop astern to effect repairs. These were completed at approximately 22.00 hrs.

While the repairs were going on, star-shells, snow flakes and red lights were observed ahead, at an estimated distance of 15 miles, and two powerful explosions, presumably depth charges, made the s.s. "YORK TOWN" shudder.

Owing to what was going on ahead of the course, the Captain decided to steer 20 miles N. of the convoy track and then run parallel to the convoy course, and meet at the rendezvous, as soon as reasonably possible.

At about this time the snowflake rocket on the s.s. "YORK TOWN" detonated spontaneously, owing, it is thought, to the rope lanyard being too taut.

On the following day, 26.9.42, when the ship was proceeding at an average speed of 12.3 knots, a torpedo struck her on the port side, under the bridge, at 20.50 hrs.

Date	- 26.9.42.
Time	- 20.50 hrs.
Speed	- 12.3 knots.
Position	- Approx. 56°50' N, 20°50' W (Moon)
Sea	- High, with heavy westerly swell.
Wind	- W.N.W. Force 8 to 9.
Visibility	- Moderate.

The attack came from two points abaft the port beam, and the hit caused the total collapse of all the superstructure along the port side. The ship sank in 90 seconds.

All the boats were swung out, but only two eventually got away, one of which capsized. Informant was pulled out of the sea on to the top of the Bridge House which was floating clear of the ship, and was later pulled on to a raft in charge of the Third Officer.

On 27.9.42 ..../

On 27.9.42, on a friendly aircraft appeared at 15.00 hours, when oil was spread from the raft to give him some idea of their set and drift. The aircraft signalled their position to a destroyer which, on the night of 28.9.42 eventually picked the survivors up.

No enemy or other aircraft was seen during either of the attacks, but on 24.9.42, an enemy homing signal was intercepted by one of the escort vessels, and a signal was sent out by the Commodore "Expect submarine attack tonight; we are being shadowed".

Informant is of the opinion that the accidental detonating of the snow-flake rocket gave away the ship's position, and that they were subsequently trailed by the U-boat which finally sank them.

Distribution:

S.I.O. Coastal Command.
D. A.S. W.
N.C.3.

93

CONFIDENTIAL

H/R.
T.D.139.1505.
16th October, 1942.

SHIPPING CASUALTIES SECTION - TRADE DIVISION.

REPORT OF AN INTERVIEW WITH THE MASTER, CAPTAIN W. P. BOYLAN.

S.S. YORKTOWN.   1,547 Gross Tons.

CONVOY. R.B. 1.   Sunk by torpedo from
                                                U-boat on 26th Sept-
                                                ember, 1942.

CAPTAIN W.P.BOYLAN.

We were bound from St. Johns (N.F.) to Londonderry in ballast.
We were armed with 1 - 12 pdr., 4.Oerlikons and 4 P.A.C.Rockets. The
Confidential Books were in a weighted bag and went down with the ship. The
number of crew, including 5 Naval and 5 Military Gunners, was 62, of whom the
2nd Engineer was injured and 18 are missing, including the 2nd Officer, 4th
Engineer, Chief W/T Officer, 1 Naval and 1 Military Gunner.

2..   We left St. Johns, N.F. on 21st September at 1400 sailing in
a special convoy R.B.1. There were 8 ships in this convoy which was sailing
in 4 columns and our position was No. 31.

3.   Nothing of incident occurred until the afternoon of 24th September
when the Commodore made a signal that we were being shadowed by a submarine
and that we could expect an attack during the night. No attack developed
and we proceeded without incident until about 1400 on 25th September when the
Commodore's ship the BOSTON was struck by 2 torpedoes on the port side, blew
up and sank in about 7 minutes. While this ship was sinking the tracks of 2
torpedoes were seen one passed ahead of us and the other one astern. I
immediately put the helm hard over to starboard, and one torpedo passed about
30 ft. ahead of my ship and one about 15 ft. from the stern. The PRESIDENT
WARFIELD, No. 41 in the convoy was firing at the torpedoes with her 12 - pdr
and machine guns.

4.   After this attack the convoy scattered and the 2 Destroyer
Escorts circled and commenced dropping depth charges. About 1600 on the
same day the convoy was reformed and the Vice Commodore in the NEW YORK took
charge. We reformed into 4 columns and I took up position as the leading
ship of the outside port column.

5.   We proceeded without further incident until 2000 on the 25th
September when the chains of my steering gear became fouled on the drum of
the steering engine and we were forced to stop to effect repairs. The
Engineers went below to effect repairs when about 2100 two violent explosions
                                                       which ....

which seemed to take place on our starboard side were both felt and heard.
The explosions were almost simultaneous and I think they took place very
close to the ship and were probably caused by two torpedoes exploding
at the end of their run. I immediately went on deck and could see snow
flakes and gun flashes from the convoy which was now about 12 miles
away.

6.   By 2200 the steering gear was repaired and I decided not to
keep to the convoy track, but steered North for about 30 miles and at 2330
25th September I altered course to pick up the straggler's route.

7.   Everything went well until 2200 G.M.T. (2050 Convoy time) on the
26th September when in position 55° 10'N. - 18° 50'W. we were struck by
a torpedo on the port side immediately underneath the bridge. The sea at
the time was very rough with a high swell and wind W.N.W. force 6, the sky
was overcast and visibility was about 2 miles. The degaussing was on at the
time and we were proceeding at 12½ knots on a course 081° (true).

8.   I was in my room lying down and everything collapsed around me
and I had great difficulty in struggling out through the mass of debris.
When I got on deck I found that all the superstructure forward of the bridge
which was made of wood had collapsed, including the bridge. The engines
had stopped immediately and very soon after I reached the deck the ship
began to crack and rend which I thought was No. 2 bulkhead giving way. The
ship sank within about 3 minutes.

9.   The starboard 'midships boat was lowered but for some unknown
reason it promptly capsized; but fortunately there was nobody in it. We
tried to get No. 1 boat away but the davits were twisted and it was
impossible to do so.

10.   The ship sank so rapidly that there was no time to get to any
of the boats and I had to jump into the water and was swimming about for an
hour until I saw a raft and swam towards it. The Chief Engineer and Fireman
were on this raft and they quickly pulled me on to it. From this raft we
could see many red lights in the water, so we commenced to paddle around
and by 1500 had taken 19 men on to our raft. The last man to be picked up
was the 2nd Wireless Operator and by this time the raft was so crowded that
this man said he preferred to stay where he was hanging on to a piece of wooden
deck house which had floated off the ship. Very few of the crew were
wearing their lifebelts as the ship had sunk very quickly and before they had
time to collect them.

11.   When daylight came I could see three other rafts floating about
The Mate and 3rd Mate who were on one of these rafts with about 12 men
pulled over to us. We saw another raft with only 3 men on it, so the Mate
said he would paddle over and bring it over to us, after which we could
even out the numbers on each raft. The Mate managed to get to this other
raft, but owing to the heavy sea he was unable to tow it back again. I
think there were also 2 men on a 4th raft, but they were too far away to be
able to get to them.

12.   Some of the crew who were still left in the water got hold of a
water logged boat, righted it and managed to bale it out dry. Eleven men got
into this boat and they picked up the 2 men from the fourth raft and took
the provisions from the raft.

13.   At noon on 27th September we were still crowded on our raft when
a large 4-engined bomber flew over us, which looked like a Flying Fortress. It
came down and circled round us and a "Mae West" with provisions was dropped to
each raft, but as we were unable to paddle over to it owing to the large number
of men on the raft we did not get our parcel. This aircraft remained with
us until about 1400.

                                                      14 ....

95

14.   We remained on the rafts for the remainder of the 27th
September and at daylight on 28th September we found that a fireman had
died during the night.

15.   About 1900 on 28th September the Destroyer SARDONIX arrived
and picked us up after we had been on the raft for 48 hours. When we
got on board this destroyer everything possible was done for us, and
nothing was too much trouble. We proceeded on board H.M.S. SARDONIX and
landed at Londonderry on the 29th September.

16.   We had water and biscuits on the rafts and also some
chocolate and a small tin of Horlicks malted milk tablets. I gave the
men 1 dipper of water three times a day and our evening meal consisted
of chocolate, Horlicks malted milk tablets and biscuits.

17.   We had no means of attracting attention on the raft, but
the men in the boat fired a Very pistol which was seen from the destroyer.

18.   All the men on the raft behaved remarkably well indeed throughout this very terrible ordeal and I have nothing but the highest praise
for them.

96

MERCHANT NAVY INTERVIEW SECTION (D.E.M.S.)

REPORT OF INTERVIEW WITH THE MASTER, CAPTAIN J. BECKETT, O.B.E.

S.S. NORTHLAND.	2,055 gross tons.
CONVOY R.B.1.	ATTACK ON CONVOY BY SUBMARINES ON THE 24th SEPTEMBER, 1942.

CAPTAIN BECKETT:

We were bound from St. John's to Londonderry in ballast, and armed with a 12 pdr. 4 Oerlikons, 4 P.A.C. Rockets, 1 Rifle and smoke floats. The ship was degaussed and switched on. My crew, including 5 Naval, 5 Army gunners and myself numbered 61. There were no casualties.

2.   We left St. John's at 1400 on the 23rd September, 1942, and proceeded in convoy with 7 other ships formed up in 4 columns, 2 ships line ahead and 4 abreast, our position being rear ship of the second starboard column. The Commodore was leading ship in the second port column, the Vice Commodore being the leading ship of the port column. The convoy was disposed 3 cables abreast and 4/5 stem and stern and was making a speed of 12 knots steering a course S.E. by E. ½ E. Our compasses were not sufficiently accurate to steer by degrees so we had to steer by points. We were escorted by two destroyers, VETERAN and VANOC disposed port and starboard of the convoy.

3.   We proceeded without incident until approximately 1400 ?. on the 24th September when in position 54° 25'N. 28° 16'W, the convoy was attacked by a submarine. The sea was moderate, wind force 2 and visibility good. I did not see or hear anything of the approach of the submarine and to my knowledge I do not think any other ships did either. The first I knew was that the Commodore Ship - BOSTON - had been struck by two torpedoes, one on the port quarter and the other on the port bow, the explosions of which threw up a huge column of water, and the vessel sunk within 4 minutes of being hit. She was an American ship and had been taken over and was now sailing under the British flag. Her gross tonnage was 5,000. I assumed that the submarine had come in from the port side and was in between the two port columns.

4.   I put my helm to port in case there should be another enemy submarine on the port side thereby reducing the target. We fired a few rounds in the direction where I thought the submarine was and then I could see the rear ship in the outside port column, NEW BEDFORD, which had been appointed Rescue Ship at a Conference held before we left, proceeding to pick up survivors from the torpedoed ship. I turned completely round, fell out of line of the convoy and went to see if I could be of any assistance, but did not bring any survivors on board. Four lifeboats were seen to be got away from the BOSTON but from what I gathered from one of the survivors later only two of the crew of the Commodore ship went on board the Rescue Ship, the remainder appeared to prefer to go over to one of the destroyers, their reason being it was an easier ship to board than the Rescue Ship. This destroyer was later sunk by enemy action. In the meantime the destroyers

had /

DISTRIBUTION:

C in C, Western Approaches.
M.H.G.
N.I.D.
D.T.L.(D.E.M.S.)
D.M/S.W.
D.T.S.D.
D.T.M.I.

DiPID. (Cdr. Edwards)
N.I.D. (Cdr. Robertson MacDonald)
D.O.D.
D.G.D.
D.N.O. (London)
Mr. R. Allen, Foreign Office.
Files.

S.S. NORTHLAND.

had closed in and the VANOC signalled me to rejoin the convoy.

5.   When I had got within three miles of the convoy - I had left the
VANOC and the NEW BEDFORD astern of me - a submarine was seen to surface some
1,500 yards from my port bow, at about 2045 Z. on the 24th September. We
were then in position 54° 36'N 26° 18'W. It appeared to be about a 740 ton
vessel, rusty in colour - no doubt from long service, and from the silhouettes
we were shown I should say it was a U-37. We immediately opened fire with
our Oerlikons and 12 pdr. I had the Army gunners manning the Oerlikon and the
Naval gunners on the 12 pdr. and the Corporal in Charge of the Oerlikon opened
fire first giving lead to the 12 pdr. crew. It is my opinion that the Naval
ratings did not see the submarine until the Oerlikon guns went into action and
from my position on the bridge I definitely saw the tracers from one of the
Oerlikons enter the enemy amidships on the third burst, although the first
and second rounds fell short. The submarine crash-dived as a result of
being hit.

6.   After the attack we stood on to rejoin the convoy and the Vice
Commodore signalled me to take up station on the port side. They had
reduced speed to 8 knots to allow the NEW BEDFORD to catch up but as arrangements had been made to increase speed at 2100 Z. the Rescue Ship was left
behind. We were still zig-zagging and I am of the opinion that the Vice
Commodore made a vital mistake here in making the zig-zag course too regular,
as I think the submarines took bearings of each leg and the time of our turns.

7.   We had a further attack by submarines at about 2050 Z. the next day,
but I did not see anything of the enemy. The first intimation I had of an
attack was an explosion on the port side of the YORKTOWN when a torpedo
entered the vessel. We had been working our D/F and about 4 minutes before
the explosion my Wireless Operator had told me he had received a signal L/W,
but could not make out the bearing. No guns went into action during this
attack, and we then parted company with the convoy and proceeded independently,
steering a Northerly course, my idea being that as this last attack had come
from the North I would be reducing my target by turning my ship in that
direction. Immediately after the attack my Wireless Operator again reported
a very strong signal, this time it was L.L/W. but he still could get no
bearing as it was too loud. I therefore took evasive action and increased
my speed to 16 knots. I adopted a mean course of N.E. steering 4 points to
Starboard and 2 points to Port, and then right ahead of me I sighted two
bright lights, very much like masthead lights, however, I knew no ship in
the convoy had masthead lights and guessed it was most probably a submarine
trying to trick me into showing my lights. I altered course to the South,
continuing to work my D/F and still picking up homing signals and call signs
from submarines. I was not given a straggler's route, it was omitted for
some unknown reason when I sailed, but I understand that route is 35°N. and
35°S. of a track running from St. John's to Malin Head.

8.   We continued working North and South of this track until the 26th
September, having been followed the whole time by a submarine believed to be
C.C.7 which we picked up on our D/F. Every evening at about sunset we would
get C.C.7 right astern of us and then another one OO5. I decided that if we
were to get away from the enemy we would have to increase our speed but much
difficulty was experienced in getting the firemen to work. At one time our
speed went down to as little as 9 knots and as I pointed out to them unless
we made all the speed possible we could not hope to save ourselves and clear
the enemy. However, after rounding up the firemen (they were all British)
we managed to make 16 knots again, and gradually drew away from the submarine
infested area, taking evasive action the whole time and picking up these
signals every evening; we got the last one when just North of Inishtrahull.

9.   I am of the opinion that at one time there were about 16 enemy submarines in the vicinity, 4 packs of 4. I do not think they could have made
duplicate signals at all as they could not have covered the ground in the
time. However, we finally cleared them and continued on our course for
Londonderry. The first ship to make port was the NAUSHON, I spoke to the
Master of this vessel and he told me he had stuck to the track having taken

98

no /

3

S.S. NORTHLAND.

no evasive action, which accounts for the fact that he got in before me.

10.   My vessel, S.S. NORTHLAND, was of the 1911 class, and used to run from Washington down to Norfolk as a pleasure steamer.   The defensive equipment was installed at Baltimore.   During this last passage 4 rounds were expended from the 12 pdr. and 30 from the Oerlikon.

11.   I have been through two or three short courses in Gunnery, also my Chief Officer.   The Second Officer was appointed Gunnery Officer, but he seemed rather lacking in experience.   Two of the M.N. Gunners were receiving the extra 6d. a day gunnery allowance, but to my knowledge none of the crew had been through any Gunnery training.   Drill is carried out periodically but this is arranged between the Senior deckhand and the Second Mate.   They usually wait until another ship is firing her guns then they use her bursts as a target and try to hit them.   We did try once to throw a barrel with a stick and flag on it overboard, using that as a target but more often than not we lost sight of it in the rise and fall of the sea.

12.   As regards the behaviour of my crew, although a very young crowd of men they were all well disciplined and appeared extremely keen and eager to do their very best.

13.   I received the O.B.E. in 1940, as a result of an action with the enemy which occurred in the North Sea when I was serving in the YEW ARCH.   We were attacked by an enemy aircraft and two bombs were dropped in very close proximity to the vessel, severely damaging it.   My gun crews were all wounded and I was left to fight the enemy alone, going to the strip Lewis gun and opening fire I was responsible for the destruction of the 'plane.   We had a Holman Projector on board but I do not think they are of much service in action.

_____

14.   Before the last war I was serving my time with my Grandfather in a sailing bark, off the Fishing Ground, Newfoundland.   When the war broke out I came to the U.K. and volunteered for service joining up with the Royal Navy as an Ordinary Seaman.   When volunteers were called for for a special job I was the only one in my ship to stand forward and was later drafted to H.M.S. FRESH HOPE, a 'Q' ship, this vessel being a fore and aft 3 masted schooner.

_____

TD/DEMS 4072/42.
20th October, 1942.

MERCHANT NAVY INTERVIEW SECTION (D.E.M.S.)

REPORT OF INTERVIEW WITH THE MASTER, CAPTAIN J. WILLIAMS.

S.S. SOUTHLAND.   2,081 gross tons.

CONVOY R.B.1.   ATTACK ON CONVOY BY
                                   SUBMARINES 25TH SEPTEMBER,
                                   1942.

CAPTAIN WILLIAMS:

We were bound from Baltimore to the U.K. in ballast and were armed with a 12 Pdr., 4 Oerlikons, 4 P.A.C. Rockets, 10 Smoke Floats and 1 Ross Rifle. The ship was degaussed and switched on. The crew, including 5 Naval and 6 Army gunners and myself, numbered 60. There were no casualties.

2. We left Baltimore at 1400 on the 3rd September, 1942, in company with 7 other ships escorted by two destroyers disposed on our port and starboard beams respectively. The convoy was formed up in 2 columns of 4, 3 cables abreast and 2/3 cables stem and stern, our vessel taking up position as second ship in the starboard wing column. Before proceeding to the U.K. (suggested destination Londonderry) we called at New York, Boston, Halifax and then St.Johns where we received our routeing instructions. Later the convoy was reformed into single line abreast, my vessel still remaining outside ship on the starboard side.

3. On the 23rd September we received a signal from the Commodore to the effect that submarines were in the vicinity and on the following day, 24th, a further message came through which stated "Enemy submarines following - expect attack tonight". However, no attack developed that night, but at 1330 the next day, 25th September, when approximately 850 miles West of Ireland, the Commodore ship, BOSTON, 2nd ship on the port side, was struck by torpedoes on her port bow and starboard quarter and sank within 9 minutes of being hit. There was a moderate sea, wind force 2/3 and visibility good. We were making a speed of 11 knots and steering on an Easterly course.

4. At the time my vessel was a little ahead of her station and being approximately 18 cables off from the Commodore ship it is difficult to say what actually happened but it is possible that she was slightly astern of the other ships in the convoy and open to attack from abaft the Vice Commodore who was abreast of her on the port side. The vessel YORKTOWN fired one shot from her 12 Pdr. but I am unable to say what she was firing at as I saw no sign of any submarines or torpedoes. No signals were received as our D/F could not pick up any bearings as it had not been insulated. We had to leave the States with it incomplete and were informed accordingly before we left port, otherwise we should have missed the convoy and probably had to stay out there all the winter owing to our class of ship - a coasting pleasure vessel - having to be built up specially to sea-worthy condition to cross

the/...

DISTRIBUTION: the/...

D. of C. Western Approaches.   D.P.D. (Cdr.Edwards)
D.A.W.G.   N.I.D. (Cdr.Robertson Macdonald)
D.T.D.   D.C.D.
D.T.D. (D.E.M.S.)   D.G.D.
—D.A/S.W.   D.N.O. (London)
D.T.S.D.   Mr.R.Allen, Foreign Office.
D.T.M.I.   Files.

the Atlantic. It was arranged, however, that all the ships that had their D/F apparatus installed and in working order should keep R.D/F watches.

5.   The Rescue ship, NEW BEDFORD and our two escorting destroyers went to the assistance of the BOSTON to pick up survivors. Several boats from the BOSTON were already away, while others were still hanging in the falls. I was later informed by the Captain of the NEW BEDFORD that when lowering one of his boats it caught underneath the belting and capsized, tipping the Chief Officer who was in charge of it into the sea; he was afterwards picked up by one of the destroyers. The Captain also told me that only two survivors came aboard his vessel, the remainder preferring to be picked up by the destroyers.

6.   By this time the convoy had become somewhat scattered and the Vice Commodore ship took up station as Commodore, sending out a signal for the ships to reform, after which we stood on our course again. Twenty minutes later I sighted the periscope of a submarine 200 - 300 yards off our starboard beam. I immediately swung the ship round to bring it astern and carried on on a zig-zag of my own, going hard to starboard and then to port. Speed was increased to 13 knots, but as this was forcing the ship, our maximum speed being 12½ knots, steam naturally fell and we got back to normal. The other vessels also increased speed but the formation and station keeping of the convoy was not good. We opened fire with our 12 Pdr. and got away 14 rounds after which we lost sight of the enemy. I did not see the submarine again but shortly after we had ceased firing the gunners saw a periscope appear on the port quarter. Eighteen more rounds were fired when the enemy disappeared from view and was not seen again. Whether it was the same submarine or not I am unable to say. The firing from our 12 Pdr. was very very rapid and I remarked afterwards that I had never seen anything quite so rapid before. Although the first shots fired were wide, the others did not seem to be too far away from the target.

7.   After this incident the convoy slowed down and stood on at a speed of 7 - 8 knots in order to allow the Rescue ship and escort vessels to catch up with us.

8.   At 2100 on the 25th September the Vice Commodore ship, S.S. NEW YORK was torpedoed and sunk. I saw the flash as the torpedo hit the ship, but did not hear the explosion, neither did I hear an explosion when the Commodore ship was sunk; the vessel then appeared to catch fire. Flares were put up by the destroyers but owing to it being so dark I could not say how long it was before the NEW YORK sank. We were doing 9 knots at the time, but I immediately increased speed and carried on on the route, zig-zagging all the time. I received no orders or signals for the convoy to disperse, but in spite of this no other vessel was to be seen.

9.   Later, while on one of my port legs of the zig-zag, I came across the Rescue ship, NEW BEDFORD. I immediately reduced speed and took up my position on her port side and kept station with her; we then carried on together. The following morning, 26th September, I sighted a destroyer astern of me on the port quarter 4 - 5 miles away. It appeared to be coming straight in our direction, but the mist came down and we lost sight of him.

10.   While proceeding in company with the NEW BEDFORD I signalled her Captain and asked whether he intended to call at Londonderry or carry on to the Clyde. Previously on the 23rd September I had received a signal from the Commodore asking me for the quantity of coal I had leaving and the amount on board at the

time/...

time, this information to be reported by noon the following day. The next morning I received a further signal asking if I had sufficient coal to reach the Clyde. After the Chief Engineer had measured the coal (there being no details available on board regarding the amount supplied) I was able to signal the Commodore to the effect that we had enough to make the Clyde. In view of the Commodore's last signal the Captain of the NEW BEDFORD and myself assumed that the Clyde was our correct destination and we decided to proceed there accordingly.

11. We stood on, but while off the West Coast of Ireland, just before coming into Inishtrahull we lost the NEW BEDFORD in the dark and had to carry on independently. We passed the NAUSHON, one of the ships which had been in the convoy, waiting for daylight in order to enter Londonderry and later saw the NEW BEDFORD again when we came into the Clyde. My ship went up to the boom and anchored for examination, after which we proceeded to D.5 anchorage. I then went ashore and made a verbal report concerning the actions to the Naval Authorities and then returned to my ship. Eventually further sailing orders were received and we proceeded independently to Loch Ewe where we joined a convoy proceeding to Methil; from there we were routed to London.

12. It seems to me that when the Commodore and Vice Commodore ships were torpedoed in both instances it happened at the time when the convoy had altered course on the zig-zag 40° to port and the vessels were open to attack.

13. The gunners behaved very well indeed and while on passage were most energetic in organising gun drill. The gunlayer was a real live wire and was exceptionally good. I have been through Part I of the long gunnery course but I could not say whether any of my Officers have taken it. No particular Officer was appointed for gunnery duties. The crew were a scratch lot who had been signed on in Baltimore when I took command of the ship, so I could not say how long they had been together. One of them had, however, been through the gunnery course and was certificated and assisted in manning the guns, although he was not signed on as a gunner.

14. Throughout the passage I had two lookouts on Monkey Island, two Naval gunners on the 12 Pdr., two Soldiers on the Oerlikons and a man at the wheel, but as soon as any trouble started the whole guns crew were immediately at their stations. We tested the guns twice from Baltimore to New York, firing 5 rounds from each of the Oerlikons and 2 rounds from the 12 Pdr. but no other opportunity occurred for any more gunnery practise during the remainder of the voyage.

15. Before going over in the QUEEN MARY to take command of the SOUTHLAND and bring her to U.K. I was one of the Coast Line Captains on the Belfast run in the Imperial Line Service. I have been on the Coast since 1933, but apart from 'blitzes' have only been in one other action.